Contents

Editorial 2
Suzanne Williams and Rachel Masika

Crossing borders and building bridges: the Baltic Region Networking Project 10
Carolina Johansson Wennerholm

Who gets to choose? Coercion, consent, and the UN Trafficking Protocol 20
Jo Doezema

Human rights or wrongs? The struggle for a rights-based response to trafficking in human beings 28
Ann D. Jordan

Trafficking in children in West and Central Africa 38
Mike Dottridge

Child marriage and prostitution: two forms of sexual exploitation? 43
Susanne Louis B. Mikhail

Slavery and gender: women's double exploitation 50
Beth Herzfeld

Half-hearted protection: what does victim protection really mean for victims of trafficking in Europe? 56
Elaine Pearson

NGO responses to trafficking in women 60
Marina Tzvetkova

A tale of two cities: shifting the paradigm of anti-trafficking programmes 69
Smarajit Jana, Nandinee Bandyopadhyay, Mrinal Kanti Dutta, and Amitrajit Saha

Reducing poverty and upholding human rights: a pragmatic approach 80
Meena Poudel and Ines Smyth

Resources 87
Compiled by Nittaya Thiraphouth
- **Publications 87**
- **Organisations 92**
- **Electronic resources 94**
- **Videos 94**
- **Conferences 95**

Editorial

Suzanne Williams and Rachel Masika

Trafficking and slavery are areas of human experience that are highly complex and which evoke powerful and contradictory feelings amongst those attempting to understand them. Slavery itself is something we like to consign to the dark period of colonial history, but it is still, uncomfortably, with us. Today it takes on a broader and more clandestine range of relationships that are less characteristic of the slave trading of previous centuries. Ordinary people are alarmed to discover that they may be implicated in slavery by becoming part of a commercial chain which exploits the bonded labour of children in the carpet industry; or by buying chocolate produced from cocoa worked by enslaved labourers in West Africa.

One aspect of modern slavery which elicits particular revulsion is the trafficking of women, girls, and boys into the sex industry, and this is one of the issues upon which many of the contributors here focus. This raises the issue of gender discrimination and oppression, and the ways in which gendered power converges with poverty to drive or lure women and girls into situations where they are subjected to extreme forms of violence. It also raises questions about women's agency and empowerment, and tests the hypocrisies of moral judgements and double standards in relation to women's and men's sexuality and identity.

Amongst national and international organisations seeking to intervene on behalf of – or in partnership with – trafficked people there exist deep divisions, on issues of principle, perception, and strategy. These divisions relate especially to two issues – the fine line between trafficking and migration, and the distinction between 'free' and 'forced' prostitution.[1] These distinctions have important consequences for the protection of the human rights of trafficked persons in receiving countries, and for the free movement of people through assisted voluntary migration. This debate is explored in several articles. It is also the case that the voices of the women, children, and men who are enslaved, traded, and trafficked, and their accounts of their experiences, vary enormously in accordance with differences in their national context, their societies, and their expectations of life. As this collection will show, there is no single truth here, but a wide range of different perceptions, contexts, and strongly-held convictions. However, there are common elements in the factors which expose people to trafficking and slavery-like practices, which define the coercion and exploitation that characterises these practices, and which form the basis of strategies to address them. These elements include inequality and oppression based on gender, age, race and caste, poverty and the struggle to overcome it, deception, corruption, and greed.

Over the past 50 years a number of international instruments have been created to deal directly or indirectly with the various elements of slavery and trafficking, starting with the Universal Declaration of Human Rights (UDHR). The UDHR states in its opening articles that: '*Everyone has the right to life, liberty and security of person. No one shall be held in slavery and servitude; slavery and the slave trade shall be prohibited in all their forms.*' (Human Rights Web 1997, Articles 3 and 4) The Convention against Torture, the Convention on the Rights of the Child, the Convention On The Elimination Of All Forms Of Discrimination Against Women (CEDAW), and the Declaration on the Elimination of Violence against Women all attempt to state and regulate the rights and duties of human beings, as individuals and in society. The 1926 Slavery Convention was supplemented in 1956 by the Supplementary Convention on the Abolition of Slavery and the Slave Trade and Institutions and Practices Similar to Slavery, and expanded the definition of slavery to those acts having the same effects as slavery, such as debt bondage, serfdom, and exploitation of the labour of women and children.

The 1949 Convention for the Suppression of the Trafficking in Persons and Exploitation of the Prostitution of Others (the Trafficking Convention), building upon international instruments concerning 'white slave traffic', brought prostitution and trafficking into the same legal framework, requiring states parties to punish those exploiting the prostitution of others, even with their consent. The contradictions inherent in this Convention continue to fuel debates about trafficking and prostitution today. The Trafficking Convention also calls upon states parties to provide care and maintenance for victims of trafficking and to bear the cost of repatriation to the nearest border. Since 1949, the definition of trafficking of women and girls was broadened to include other forms of exploitation such as forced marriage and forced labour, reflected in the Beijing Declaration and Platform for Action.

Finally, in the year 2000, all countries signed the UN Convention against Transnational Organised Crime and its two protocols. One of the protocols deals specifically with trafficking in persons – the Protocol to Prevent, Suppress and Punish Trafficking in Persons, Especially Women and Children. The Protocol provides the first international definition of trafficking. This definition broadens that of the 1949 Convention, which set prostitution at the heart of trafficking, and bound states parties to 'take all necessary measures to repeal or abolish any law, regulation or administrative provisions by virtue of which persons who are engaged in, or are suspected of engaging in, prostitution are subject either to special registration or to the possession of a special document or to any exceptional requirements for supervision or notification'. Advocates of this 'abolitionist' system emphasise effective legislation against illicit traffic and exploitation of the traffic of others, drafted to preclude traffickers and profiteers from circumventing them and escaping punishment. There is no distinction between forced and voluntary prostitution.

The definition of trafficking in the UN protocol (UNODCCP 2000) reads:

'"Trafficking in persons" shall mean the recruitment, transportation, transfer, harbouring or receipt of persons, by means of the threat or use of force or other forms of coercion, of abduction, of fraud, of deception, of the abuse of power or of a position of vulnerability (interpretative note 63) or of the giving or receiving of payments or benefits to achieve the consent of a person having control over another person, for the purpose of exploitation. Exploitation shall include, at a minimum, the exploitation of the prostitution of others or other forms of sexual exploitation (interpretative note 64),

forced labour or services, slavery or practices similar to slavery, servitude or the removal of organs.'

Interpretative note 64 circumvents the issue of different national legal approaches to prostitution, by stating that the protocol addresses the exploitation of the prostitution of others only in the context of trafficking, and avoiding a definition of prostitution itself. By making coercion and deception central to the definition of trafficking, it does not require governments to consider all prostitution to be trafficking, and thus illegal. What the Protocol fails to do, however, is to require signatories to extend assistance and human rights protection to trafficked persons.

The discussion and debates which surrounded the defining of trafficking during the drawing up of the protocol reflected the polarised positions of many of the governmental and non-governmental organisations involved in the process. Several authors in this collection address these debates. Jo Doezema discusses the arguments put forward by two broad lobby groups at the negotiations. The Human Rights Caucus views focuses on the rights of trafficking victims. It recognises the difference between forced and voluntary prostitution, presenting sex work as a legitimate labour option for women, one in which women have agency, and for which they should not be penalised, morally or legally. The Coalition Against Trafficking in Women (CATW), problematises prostitution in itself as an extreme form of gender discrimination, and thus as a violation of women's fundamental human rights.

A key difference between these two broad coalitions rests on the notion of consent and whether women can meaningfully consent to sex work, or are always coerced into prostitution by virtue of the gendered nature of sexual relations, by force, or as the result of limited options for earning a living. Doezema traces the historical context of the debates on the notions of consent and coercion, and shows how the compromise around consent in the protocol leaves the interpretation of what it actually means to the discretion of states parties. This entails that when the protocol is translated into law and policy, initiatives may be either repressive or emancipatory for women, depending on the state's interpretation.

Ann Jordan also provides an historical overview of the development of international law on trafficking, and points to the negative consequence of the conflation of trafficking with prostitution in the Trafficking Convention of 1949, that of criminalising prostitutes and their clients. As long as national legal systems follow this model, there are considerable dangers for women involved in prostitution. For example, they may be forced into the hands of third parties offering protection from arrest and police abuse in exchange for the proceeds of, or control over, sex workers' labour. Once the industry is pushed underground, organised crime takes over, and sex work continues or increases under more violent conditions. Jordan argues that a human rights approach to trafficking provides a better framework for tackling trafficking because it upholds the rights of the victims.

The conditions faced by trafficked persons include classic elements associated with slavery historically, such as abduction, use of false promises, transport to a strange city or country, loss of freedom and personal dignity, extreme physical abuse, and deprivation. The persistent oppression of women, and the vulnerability of children, intersecting with other forms of discrimination such as poverty, caste, and race, means they are over-represented among trafficked and bonded persons. The International Organisation for Migration (IOM) estimates that between 700,000 and two million women and children are trafficked across international borders annually (IOM 2001, 1).

Accurate numbers are difficult to obtain due to the clandestine and illegal nature of trafficking, the lack of anti-trafficking legislation in many countries, the reluctance of victims to report their experiences to the authorities, and the lack of government priority given to data collection and research. Whilst a large proportion of women and children are trafficked for the purpose of prostitution, men, women, and children are trafficked for other purposes that include entertainment, sweatshop industries, illegal adoption of children, organ transplants, forced marriage, mail-order brides, domestic work, forced labour, drug trafficking, and begging.

What drives women, men, and children to leave their homes and take unknown risks at the hands of traffickers? What compels parents to send their children away from home? What mechanisms, factors, and forces make it possible for some people to exercise ownership rights over others? To what extent does trafficking or sex work involve consent, choice, or coercion? Where do we draw a line distinguishing between migration and trafficking? What are the implications of the new UN Protocol for trafficked persons? What does 'protection' mean for trafficked persons? Do current responses and measures incorporate the specific needs of trafficked women, especially those suffering gender-based violence? Does trafficking in women perpetuate and reinforce the subordinate status of women?

This collection of articles explores and debates these questions, from a range of perspectives. The writers highlight the different understandings of the issues, the incentives to migrate, the realities that trafficked persons confront, and the inherent complexities in dealing with the outcomes. They emphasise the need for a multitude of multi-agency responses that incorporate human rights considerations and tackle poverty and unequal gender relations.

What facilitates trafficking and slavery?

Globalisation, dislocation, and poverty

Globalisation, liberalisation, and free market promotion have paved the way for the unfettered movement of capital and labour. While borders have opened for trade, capital, investors, and individuals from wealthier countries, people from poorer countries have not been given the same freedom of movement. Many Western nations have introduced stringent restrictions and prohibitive immigration laws to keep out asylum seekers and economic migrants from poorer countries.

Within this climate of immigration restrictions, trafficking has flourished, and more people are turning to traffickers to facilitate migration. Carolina Wennerholm provides a brief overview of the extent of trafficking, citing Asia and the Baltic Region to show how the majority of trafficked persons are women. Patterns of movement are varied, occurring within countries and across borders and continents.

People move for many reasons: they may seek better employment opportunities; safety from persecution, violence, human rights violations, discrimination, religious and cultural tensions; or an escape from poverty. Economic decline, civil wars, ethnic conflicts, and environmental disasters are all 'push factors' and may bring about a breakdown of law and order at home that makes opportunities for trafficking and bonded forms of labour easier to exploit. Children captured by the Lord's Resistance Army in Uganda, for example, have been forcibly taken to Sudan and enslaved: boys as soldiers, girls as servants, 'wives', and sex slaves (Leggett 2001).

Poverty and the aspiration for a better way of life are by far the major 'push factors' and are also among the principal reasons why parents send their children away to work. As Wennerholm points out, remittances from children's labour can sustain entire families in some Asian countries. However, Wennerholm cautions against assuming that anti-poverty strategies or economic growth on their own can eradicate the problem. In countries where there is an expanding middle class such as Indonesia, Malaysia, and the Philippines, the financial capacity and motivation for men to purchase sex services has increased. Where there is a demand for such services, trafficking in women increases.

Gender-based discrimination

While males are trafficked also, with trade in young boys dominating in some parts of the world, the majority of trafficked persons are women and girls. Trafficking is a highly gendered transaction. Unequal gender relations and patriarchal values and systems are at the root of the causes and patterns of trafficking and other forms of enslavement. In all cases, but particularly where it takes the form of violence and sexual abuse against women and girls, discrimination is a major factor behind trafficking. Key locations of discrimination include the household, the family, and the immediate community.

Because it is widely the case that girls are less valued than boys, many families make less investment in their future. In societies where dowry payments are required, or where girls leave home when they get married and no longer contribute to household income and labour, girls may be perceived to be a financial burden on families. This low-status, low investment, vicious cycle leaves women and girls with limited economic options, increases their vulnerability to highly exploitative forms of labour, and leads them to take exceptional risks. 'In some countries where discrimination against female children is more pronounced, daughters are made to feel their financial obligation to the family.' (CATW 1995, 12) Limited access to education and information for girls and women in many societies can make them easy prey for the duplicity of traffickers. Non-participation in political activity and decision-making processes limits women's ability to effect change, challenge discriminatory practices, or bring about action to prosecute traffickers.

Several authors in this collection discuss the gender discrimination that characterises trafficking and slavery-like practices in different cultural settings and country-specific contexts. Smarajit Jana *et al.* use case studies to demonstrate the ways in which gender discrimination, inequality, and cultural constraints on women in Bangladesh and India entice women into trafficking for sex work, and the discrimination and violence they encounter thereafter. Jana *et al.* also debate the role of agency, presenting the perspectives of sex workers for whom sex work is one of the few available options for self-advancement and survival.

Beth Herzfeld provides examples of gender-specific forms of slavery, such as ritual servitude in West Africa. In these cases, girls are given by their family to a shrine to atone for a family transgression. Priests exercise ownership over these girls, who are obliged to act as wives and provide sexual services to their 'owners'. Herzfeld highlights the additional hardships that women and girls face within certain forms of bonded labour, and the gendered differences in the types of work that children are forced to take on.

Meena Poudel and Ines Smyth use the case of a young Nepali woman to illustrate the elements of crime and violence involved in trafficking, and the role that social institutions such as the household, family, community, market, and state may play in violating the rights of women and girls. They provide examples of human rights violations during the three stages of trafficking – recruitment, work, and rescue.

Mike Dottridge demonstrates the way in which the common practice in West and Central Africa of sending children to wealthier relatives in cities and other countries is being distorted by poverty.

Girls are more at risk of being trafficked for domestic service because they are considered more obedient and suited for this type of work. Dotteridge concludes by reflecting that if the majority of trafficked children were boys, rather than girls, more attention would be paid to the problem.

Susanne Mikhael outlines the ways in which cultural constructions of gender roles in the Middle East and North Africa can lead to disadvantage and potentially adverse impacts on the survival, livelihood opportunities, and choices of children. Mikhael points to certain similarities between child marriage and prostitution, areas of exploitation usually considered as being very different. She describes how these practices, in different ways, violate the rights of children and perpetuate the exercise of ownership rights over individuals for the purposes of exploiting their sexuality or labour. She highlights the ways in which the cultural context underpinning these practices does not provide girls with the protection they require as children, and to which they have internationally-agreed rights.

Response strategies

Trafficking and slavery have a multi-faceted nature involving illegal migration, violence, violations of human rights and labour standards, poverty, and gender discrimination. Institutional responses to trafficking and slavery reflect this variety of concerns and are largely influenced by political considerations, organisational culture and interests, the different ways of viewing the problem and the solutions, and country-specific factors such as the existence or non-existence of anti-trafficking legal frameworks and the resources to provide for basic needs and protection.

The United Nations (UN) and other Inter-Governmental Organisations (IGOs) have dedicated substantial resources to develop more effective solutions. UNIFEM-Asia Pacific, for example, sees trafficking in women and children as a gender issue and a serious form of violence against women. Economic empowerment of women is seen as a key factor for anti-trafficking strategies in origin and resettlement countries. In conjunction with USAID, UNIFEM is implementing an anti-trafficking initiative in the Mekong sub-region (UNIFEM East and South-East Asia 2001).[2]

Ann Jordan points out that in the context of the new UN Protocol, which is very weak on protection of victims, there are opportunities for advocates to influence the process of adopting domestic anti-trafficking legislation in signatory countries. Currently, most have inappropriate or inadequate laws and policies providing some protection to victims or none at all. She cautions that conflating trafficking with undocumented migrations risks leading to the prosecution of victims while traffickers escape.

For the most part, victim protection has been prioritised only when victims assist in prosecutions. As Elaine Pearson points out in this collection, in the case of trafficked women in Western Europe, the kinds of measures undertaken by law enforcement officials in Europe can increase some women's vulnerability to discrimination and violations of their rights. Providing victims with temporary rights to stay in the country of destination with access to services such as housing, medical and legal services, counselling, language and integration courses, financial assistance, and in some countries the right to work, for the purpose of giving testimony, rewards those willing to testify and penalises those who are not.

Women returning home after having been trafficked may be shunned by their families and communities because of punitive attitudes towards women's sexuality in countries of origin. In some countries they are detained, forced to undergo compulsory medical tests, and have their identities exposed in the media.

The various needs of those who survive an experience of trafficking range from protection and legal assistance to psychological counselling, financial assistance, and shelter. Jana *et al.* and Poudel and Smyth show how trafficking creates additional hardships for women including sexual exploitation and other forms of gender-based violence and discrimination, requiring gender-responsive interventions.

Because of their illegal status, many trafficked people fear and distrust state-run organisations. For this reason, and because the majority of trafficked people are women, human rights and women's organisations have often been their first port of call. These organisations have also been very active in raising awareness, lobbying for change, and providing assistance and support services for victims. Marina Tzvetkova argues that despite the high profile of gender issues within the development and human rights sector, some well-meaning organisations treat trafficked men and women as passive victims incapable of making reasoned judgments, and needing to be rescued and rehabilitated. Jordan and Jana *et al.* argue that in reality, trafficked people may be strong, risk-taking individuals who have made rational choices and exercised their own agency in deciding to migrate.

Non-governmental organisations (NGOs) have initiated a variety of assistance programmes for trafficking victims, survivors, and those at risk at local, national, and international levels. Tzvetkova provides an overview of this NGO activity around the world, particularly that against trafficking in women for sexual exploitation. Wennerholm highlights the anti-trafficking strategies undertaken by *Kvinnoforum*, a Swedish NGO that focuses on research, information provision, and networking to raise awareness of the complexity and serious violations of human rights that characterise trafficking. Jana *et al.* present the initiatives of an HIV prevention and intervention organisation working in Bangladesh and India whose work includes outreach work with and practical support for sex workers, and political initiatives to uphold the rights of this marginalised group. Herzfeld cites an example of Anti-Slavery International's work that includes raising awareness of the harm of bonded labour and using child labour, and has had some significant results. Poudel and Smyth discuss Oxfam's anti-trafficking programme in Asia, which is rooted in a poverty reduction and rights-based framework.

Tackling the roots of poverty and oppression means looking not only at material poverty and need, but also at the poverty of rights and entitlements. This is consistent with a commitment to the empowerment of women and to their agency in achieving human rights and overcoming inequality and oppression. A rights-based poverty strategy tackles the causes of inequality, in which trafficking and slavery are rooted, and works with local, national, and international agents to achieve changes in families and communities and the national and international legal and policy agendas.

Whilst this collection demonstrates the variety of perspectives and strategies towards trafficking in people and slavery-like practices, there is a common thread. It is clear that the Trafficking Protocol and other international instruments that deal with the various elements of trafficking and slavery need to work. Those who legislate or intervene on behalf of victims, survivors, and those at risk also need to incorporate human rights considerations and initiatives to eliminate gender discrimination into their work if these practices are to end.

Suzanne Williams is a Policy Adviser at Oxfam GB, 274 Banbury Road, Oxford OX2 7DZ.
E-mail: swilliams@oxfam.org.uk

Notes

1 In this article, the terms 'prostitution' and 'sex work' are used interchangeably.
2 Personal communication with Lorraine Corner, Regional Economic Adviser, UNIFEM Asia Pacific and Arab States, 6 February 2002.

References

Coalition Against Trafficking in Women – Asia Pacific (CATW) (1995) *Trafficking in Women and Prostitution in the Asia Pacific*, Manila: CATW

Human Rights Web (1997) 'Universal Declaration of Human Rights', http://www.hrweb.org/legal/udhr.html (last checked January 2002)

International Organization for Migration (IOM) (2001), 'New global figures on the global scale of trafficking' in *Trafficking in Migrants Quarterly Bulletin* 23: April 2001, special issue, http://www.iom.int//documents/publications/en/tm_23.pdf (last checked February 2002)

Leggett, I. (2001) *Uganda: An Oxfam Country Profile*, Oxford: Oxfam GB

UNIFEM East and South-East Asia (2001) 'Trafficking in Women and Children: Mekong Sub-Region', http://www.unifem-eseasia.org/Resources/Traffick2.html (last checked January 2002)

United Nations Office for Drug Control and Crime Prevention (UNODCCP) (2000) 'The Protocol to Prevent, Suppress and Punish Trafficking in Persons', http://odccp.org//trafficking_protocol.html (last checked February 2002)

Crossing borders and building bridges: the Baltic Region Networking Project

Carolina Johansson Wennerholm

'16 year old Lithuanian girl found dead on a highway outside Malmö in southern Sweden.' She committed suicide after escaping from an apartment where she earned her living selling sexual services. 'Czech girls kept as sex slaves at a hotel outside Stockholm calling their mothers for help.' Headlines like this concerning the trafficking of women and girls occur in many countries of the world every day. Some trafficked women are seeking to improve their lives or feed their children, while others have been abducted and forced into 'slave' labour. Occurrences of violence and human rights violations are common. This article gives an overview of the reasons for, and mechanics of, trafficking.[1] It also highlights the anti-trafficking approaches and activities undertaken by the Swedish NGO Kvinnoforum in partnership with five NGOs in the Baltic Sea and Nordic Region. These projects address trafficking through research, information, and networking to create awareness of the complexity of trafficking, and the serious human rights violations that it involves.

Trafficking of women has been a feminist issue since the beginning of the 20th century when advocates for change like Josephine Butler fought against the 'white slave trade'. They recognised that women and girls have been the majority of all victims of trafficking. It is only recently that the magnitude and complexity of trafficking has increased its importance on the international agenda. This process has been assisted by a widening of focus to encompass trafficking for bonded labour in sweatshops, domestic work, adoption, and marriage, in addition to trafficking for prostitution.

The definition of trafficking in human beings has been hotly debated amongst the anti-trafficking movement. The debate reflects many differing approaches or foci. However, in December 2000 the UN adopted a definition which covered the diversity of means and mechanics used, the issue of violence and abuse of power for purposes of exploitation, as well as the many purposes for trafficking – including exploitation of others through prostitution, forced labour, and slavery-like practices, or the removal of organs.[2]

A global phenomenon

Global political and economic processes and developments influence trafficking. Economic crises and disparities between countries fuel supply, while demand for cheap labour attracts desperate migrants. Economic liberalisation relaxes controls and opens borders between countries, facilitating population mobility. Conflict, transnational crime, and political transitions and upheavals are also contributory factors.

The International Organisation for Migration has estimated that between 700,000 and two million women are trafficked across international borders annually (IOM 2001). Accurate numbers are difficult to ascertain for various reasons. Firstly, the definition of trafficking is contested. Secondly, the criminal nature of the problem has consequences for what is measured and how. Thirdly, it has not been a priority in many countries to make the problem visible.

Trafficking occurs both within domestic borders, and across countries, regions, and continents. Countries of origin, transit, and destination are intertwined and overlap. A single country may export women, girls, and boys abroad, may temporarily harbour arrivals from other countries, and act as the destination country for others.

In South and East Asia, trafficked persons originate mainly from Thailand, China, the Philippines, Burma/Myanmar, Vietnam, Cambodia, Bangladesh, and Nepal. Transit and destination countries include Thailand, Malaysia, Japan, India, and Pakistan. While the provision of workers for the sex industry is the main purpose of this traffic, women from these regions are also trafficked for domestic work and other forms of bonded labour. As a result of the burden of dowry, some women are trafficked for marriage purposes. In some communities in India and Nepal, commercial sexual services have religious and cultural links, increasing the complexity of the problem (O'Neill 1999). Trafficking in children – girls and boys – for purposes of sexual exploitation, adoption, begging and other forms of bonded labour, is mostly reported from East, South-East, and South Asia (Swedish Ministry for Foreign Affairs 2001). In Sri Lanka the majority of the children offering sexual services are boys (O'Neill 1999).

Former Soviet Union (FSU) countries in Central Asia are also origin countries. Women from Kazakhstan, Kyrgyszstan, and Tajikistan are trafficked to the Middle East, Turkey, Greece, and Ukraine (IOM 2001), often via Russia.

Trafficking has increased dramatically in Europe since the fall of the Iron Curtain in 1989. Most trafficked women come from former communist countries such as Russia, Ukraine, Albania, Kosovo, the Baltic States, the Czech Republic, and Poland, and are destined for Western European countries (IOM 2001). However, women from South-East Asia, Africa, and Latin America also arrive in Western European destinations. These women are usually involved in the sex business, and sometimes in domestic work. The international presence in the Balkans as a result of the war there has led to an increase in the demand for sex services within these countries, and an increase in the trafficking of women into countries such as Kosovo. Children are also trafficked into and within Western Europe, such as Albanian children to Greece and Italy for begging and drug-dealing (UNICEF 2000 in Swedish Ministry for Foreign Affairs 2001).

The USA is a major destination country, particularly for women and children from South-East Asia, Latin America, and increasingly from FSU countries. While again the main purposes are the sex industry and bonded labour, other trafficking industries include mail-order bride companies, maid schemes, domestic servants, and illicit foreign adoption (O'Neill 1999). Canada is a receiving country, as well as transit country for those travelling to the USA (McDonald *et al.* 2000).

Latin America has a long tradition of trafficking. Countries of origin include Dominican Republic, Colombia, Cuba, Mexico, Brazil, Ecuador, Surinam, Venezuela, Uruguay, Peru, Argentina, and Paraguay. Destination countries include mostly Western European countries, but also Japan and the USA (STV 1996). The purposes include prostitution, domestic work, and marriage.

There is growing concern over the increasing numbers of trafficked persons within and from Africa, but as yet there is little data available. Countries of origin include Ghana, Nigeria, Ethiopia, and Mali; destination countries include Nigeria, Côte d'Ivoire, Western Europe, and Middle Eastern countries – Lebanon, Libya, Kuwait, and Saudi Arabia – as well as the USA (IOM 2001). In Central and West Africa, women may be trafficked as domestic workers, and children for plantation work, domestic work, and sex services. The Middle East receives women from Africa and Central Asia. Israel has received women from Russia, Ukraine, Azerbaijan, Moldova, Kazakhstan, Turkey, the Dominican Republic, Brazil, and South Africa (Gruenpeter Gold *et al.* 2001).

Exploring the causes of trafficking

The causes of trafficking are complex, intertwined, and context-specific, with poverty and unequal gender relations as key underlying root causes. The situation of women and children in countries of origin, the profit motive, the ease with which trafficking occurs, and the demand for women and children for different exploitative purposes are principal supply and demand factors.

The situation of women, girls, and boys in countries of origin

The socio-economic and cultural context underpinning women and children's lives determines their choices, strategies, and coping mechanisms. Women's unequal rights and access to formal labour, the restricted control they exercise over their own lives, and the gendered aspects of poverty all lead women to seek work abroad. In middle and low-income countries, many women face high unemployment, low wages, lack of child care, and a high frequency of sexual harassment in the workplace as well as gender violence. Some women opt to enter the prostitution business, sometimes encouraged by their husbands. Others seek trafficking mechanisms for domestic, catering, or other work, and end up in prostitution against their will (Strandberg 1999).

Traffickers can exploit women's desire to create a better life for themselves in other countries by luring them with promises of jobs as waitresses, maids, dancers, models, and babysitters. In some cases, women answer advertisements for work in the EU, or trust 'friends of a friend' to arrange such work. Women are told that all they need to do is sign a contract, and that the expenses of the trip are to be paid when they start earning. Upon arrival, however, some women find that the promised job does not exist, and are forced to perform sexual services or take part in pornographic films, often in conditions of slavery.

Social constructions of gender relations and sexuality facilitate trafficking for sexual exploitation. Girls may feel a sense of duty to repay their parents' care and protection. In some poor rural households in South-East Asia, remittances from daughters who have entered prostitution represent the sole source of financial support (Lim 1998). Girls sold into prostitution have sometimes returned home with honour, because they brought money, goods, and security to the family (Belsey 1996, cited in Lim 1998, 13). In some areas in South-East Asia, prostitution is socially accepted as an inevitable evil 'necessary to satiate an uncontainable male sexuality' (D'Cunha 1992, 36, cited in Lim 1998, 12).

Psychological problems owing to unpleasant encounters and their social impact can drive women away from home and into prostitution. In the Philippines, unmarried women who lose their virginity – some as a result of rape – enter prostitution believing it is what they deserve (Lim 1998). Women who endure violence at home or at work, who suffer from sexual harassment, or who were sexually abused as children, may enter prostitution, and are often easy targets for traffickers (Kvinnoforum 1999).

Evidence from countries as diverse as Mali, the Baltic countries, Ukraine, Moldova, and Thailand show that some girls and women enter prostitution or seek trafficking mechanisms longing for a more materialistic life style or to participate in the urban nightlife (MAHR 2000; Diakiti 1999).

Of those who migrate for sex work, few realise that at best they will keep only a small proportion of their earnings, and most are unaware that they will be locked up, beaten, and have no control over the number and nature of services they will have to provide. Debt-bondage, violence, threats, physical bondage, guilt, and the threat of harming their families, keep women in compliance. Because they risk arrest for prostitution or illegal immigration, women seldom seek help from the police. A frequent inability to speak the local language makes these women additionally vulnerable and powerless (Strandberg 1999, 7).

In some cases, girls, boys, and women are kidnapped or abducted into the trafficking trade. In some regions, parents sell their children, and partners or relatives sell women.

Demand for services

Increasing demand for commercial sexual services in an expanding industry fuels trafficking. The argument that addressing poverty would on its own inhibit trafficking is questionable. Where economic growth has created an expanding middle class, for example in Indonesia, Malaysia, and the Philippines, the capacity and even the motivation for men to buy sexual services has increased. This has expanded the industry to the extent where aspects like age, ethnicity and race, virginity, and sexual health are key considerations for customers and thus traffickers, with increasing emphasis on trafficking younger persons who are less likely to have contracted HIV/AIDS and other STDs. Thus, to buy sexual services may in this context be seen as a lifestyle choice, which adapts to economic circumstances (Lim 1998).

Although the growth of tourism has drawn an increasing number of women and children to the sex industry in these countries, local people continue to account for most of the demand (*ibid.*). Thus, the expansion of attitudes and lifestyles where buying sex is acceptable are a key factor in the increased demand for women and children in the sex business.

Trafficking has an ethnic dimension. Minorities often experience difficulties in the formal labour market and may be discriminated against. In Estonia and Latvia, ethnic Russians find it difficult to find formal employment. As a result, there are large numbers of Russian women prostitutes in Riga and Tallinn. Similarly, Thai and Sri Lankan children from the hill tribes are trafficked for sex exploitation (Swedish Ministry for Foreign Affairs 2001). It has also been reported how modern 'slave markets' in the Balkan region contain women from a wide range of ethnic origin whose value and marketing depends largely on their skin colour, racial characteristics, and the prevailing perception about what is 'exotic'.[3]

Organised trafficking and profit

Trafficking is a lucrative business, and – unlike arms and drugs – trafficked women and children can be sold many times. The UN estimates that the trafficking industry is worth US$5-7 billion annually (CATW 2001, 1). The main beneficiaries are the various actors involved in the trafficking chain, and profits earned by pimps are often laundered.

The increase in criminal networks dealing with trafficking has a direct link with the levels of profit, the ease with which trafficking can be undertaken, and the low penalties for those caught (Europol 1999). In many cases, traffickers also deal in drugs, arms, and animals. However, it is safer to trade with human beings. It is relatively easy for traffickers to set up undercover businesses such as model and film agencies and marriage bureaux, through which women and children are contracted and traded. Women may also enter countries on a tourist visa or with a false passport. Corruption among state officials, police officers, migration staff, and others further facilitates the commerce (Kvinnoforum 1999).

Traffickers operate both within small-scale informal networks and as part of well-organised international criminal networks (Europol 1999). In Northern Europe, Russian and Estonian women cross the border to Finland, Sweden, and Norway every weekend, sometimes encouraged by husbands or other relatives. Bus drivers, hotel and camp-site owners, and pimps all earn from this. The actors in the trafficking chain may or may not know each other. However, these informal criminal networks may be as dangerous as mafia groups. In small villages where everybody knows each other, threats and harassment can have a tremendous impact on women and children, keeping them in compliance with the traffickers. The stigma that women and girls who are trafficked fear or experience may inhibit their return to their own communities if they escape.[4]

Measuring the impacts of trafficking

The impacts of trafficking on societies require further research. Communities where trafficking is frequent lose young, productive women. Where these women return, they may in turn become traffickers themselves. Negative socialisation may also become a major problem for abused children. The costs of supporting rescued women and children, and of training and prosecuting traffickers are high.

The impact of trafficking on victims, who often face unexpected harsh conditions, is better understood. For women and children trafficked into prostitution, the effects on their psychological, reproductive and sexual health, and well-being can be devastating.

Health effects

Rape and other violence, drug use, and lack of food and sleep are commonly experienced by the victims of trafficking. The consequences of these include trauma, depression, and even suicide. Women and children forced to sell sexual services risk contracting STDs and HIV / AIDS. Trafficked sex workers, many working on the street, endure violent and unsafe sex as a result of the fact that they have no negotiating position, and are often illegal immigrants. Sexual exploitation can lead to post-traumatic stress disorders as well as unwanted pregnancies and unsafe abortions, the most common reason for maternal deaths among women worldwide. Trafficked women and children also have limited or no access to healthcare services.

Social effects

Victims of trafficking transported to distant or unfamiliar surroundings are vulnerable, particularly if they do not speak the language of the destination country. These women and children become frightened and have difficulties building trust-based social relationships. Many feel that they will be stigmatised for the rest of their lives and may not wish to return home, even if they could. The children born to women in trafficking circumstances may be adopted, placed in orphanages, or abandoned.

Legal effects

Trafficked women and children often have an illegal immigration status in destination countries. Since legal frameworks relating to trafficking and prostitution vary, victims of trafficking are commonly deported without adequate support, or imprisoned. Law enforcement may trap the victim of trafficking rather the trafficker.

Economic effects

Many women undergo trafficking in order to improve their own and their family's economic situation. Where women succeed in remitting some income to their family, this encourages the sale of other women or children to the traffickers. However, in far too many instances women and children become indebted to the traffickers and have to work for years to pay back unforeseen 'contract costs'.

Kvinnoforum: the 'Crossing Borders and Building Bridges' networking project in the Baltic Region[5]

Since the break up of the FSU there has been a dramatic increase in the numbers of women travelling to Sweden from the neighbouring eastern Baltic countries. The worsening economic situation in these countries, and its gendered impact, is a contributory factor. Many women are attracted by employment opportunities in richer neighbouring countries. While some access 'normal' jobs, others are lured or forced by traffickers into the sex business.

Until recently there was little awareness of the dimensions and mechanisms of trafficking in Scandinavian and Baltic countries. Trafficking was regarded as a particularly Southern phenomenon. The increasing visibility of foreign prostitutes reported on the streets of Scandinavian cities in the last decade demonstrated to Scandinavian countries that they too had become part of the trafficking trade, with police and politicians becoming alarmed at the increasing trafficking of women and girls into a region that prided itself as one of the most gender equal in the world.

The Swedish NGO *Kvinnoforum*, which works with disadvantaged women, was alarmed by the increase in this particular manifestation of gender inequality. Kvinnoforum mobilised NGO resources to cater for the needs of these women and to publicise their plight. It conducted a survey of organisations actively working against trafficking, with the aim of finding what kinds of activities were being undertaken, and what the needs of trafficked women were, within the Nordic and Baltic States, Russia, and Belarus.[6]

The results of a questionnaire sent to NGOs, researchers, and government organisations, and interviews held with key informants indicated the following:

- a lack of awareness of trafficking in the Nordic region, despite the existence of large numbers of women and children experiencing trafficking-related human rights violations;
- a limited capacity to address trafficking, with few NGO or government actors undertaking this work;
- discrepancies and contested views on the problem and solutions;
- a need for sharing information and experiences as well as networking and co-operation;
- an increasing interest in trafficking issues and their incorporation into NGO work.

Objectives and methodology

Informed by the findings, Kvinnoforum has continued its work against trafficking in the Baltic Region with a series of projects and activities. The overall objectives are:

- to learn more about, and raise awareness of, the many dimensions of trafficking in women and children;
- to invite new actors and build a national and regional network around the Baltic Sea across organisational, geographical, and ideological borders;
- to develop strategies and specific activities to counteract trafficking and support victims, and to bridge the gap between differing ideological positions on trafficking.

Kvinnoforum employs three analytical approaches to understanding trafficking: a gender perspective, a human rights perspective, and a diversity perspective.

Gender perspective

Understanding the supply and demand aspects of trafficking is an important part of the identification of solutions. A gender perspective is a useful analytical tool for understanding why women, girls, and boys voluntarily seek or are easily lured into trafficking, and why there is a market and demand for it. Trafficking in women, girls, and boys is viewed as an outcome of unequal gender relations in both origin and destination countries. A gender analysis highlights the differences among women and between men and women in terms of needs, capabilities, vulnerabilities, and strategies, and a gender-aware approach is part of a multifaceted approach which can help us to address this complex problem at global and local levels.

Human rights perspective

The human rights perspective focuses on the violation of the individual's rights to freedom, health, development, absence of violence, and so on, and distinguishes trafficking from smuggling and illegal migration. It implies a shift to supporting victims of trafficking instead of labelling them as criminals. It provides a broad and common platform for contesting views and approaches to trafficking and prostitution,[7] and can access legislation, including International Human Rights Instruments, in many cases.

Diversity perspective

The diversity approach is closely linked to the gender perspective, recognising the heterogeneity of women and men and their different needs, vulnerabilities, capacities, and coping strategies. Diversity implies openness to social difference, which promotes tolerance and is therefore an important methodological bridging approach for a highly contested issue such as anti-trafficking work.

Diversity has in practice meant that an array of organisations, such as NGOs and governments, can collaborate as part of a network despite ideological differences. At the regional level, Kvinnoforum collaborates with NGOs from five Baltic nations incorporating very different languages, cultures, and socio-economic circumstances. Each NGO also focuses on different aspects of the problem: street work with women in prostitution, HIV/AIDS prevention, academic research, development of social work, intercultural support for women with foreign backgrounds, and strategies for women's empowerment. Locally, diverse actors such as the police, social workers, politicians, researchers, and NGO activists have attended strategy workshops to discuss trafficking and propose measures against it.

Information sharing and networking

Following the initial research, Kvinnoforum initiated partnerships with the Latvian Gender Problem Centre and Monika, the Multicultural Women's Association in Finland.[8] Three persons from each of the three organisations travelled to the Baltic and Nordic states to meet with NGOs, government representatives, and the media, to disseminate and gather information on regional trafficking in women and girls.

Publication of a resource book on trafficking in women and girls

This project identified 80 organisations working, or interested in working, against trafficking in the Baltic Region. *Trafficking in Women and Girls in the Baltic Sea Region, A Resource Book* was published in 1999. It includes articles, printed and on-line references, websites for networks and organisations, and information on all 80 organisations. It thus provides useful information for cross-border anti-trafficking work.

Local, regional, and global networking
Following this, Kvinnoforum expanded the collaboration to include NGOs in Finland, Estonia, Latvia, Lithuania, Denmark, and Sweden. These NGOs have conducted training workshops in their respective countries for central actors working against trafficking. The workshops have helped to create national networks against trafficking in each of the countries. An advantage of working in partnership is that there is more than one 'owner' of the project and its aim, thus enhancing the credibility and sustainability of the work.[9] As a joint activity, the network will update the *Resource Book*.

Each organisation further undertakes separate projects in its respective country. The Gender Problem Centre in Latvia runs a shelter for returning women and is also involved in preventive work among adolescents. The AIDS Prevention and Information Centre in Estonia provides reproductive health services and information to women in prostitution. In Lithuania, PRAEITIES PEDOS has published a book and a film on trafficking. In Finland, Monika has initiated a hotline for foreign women experiencing problems of violence. In Sweden, Kvinnoforum gives lectures and discusses training with the police and migration services. These projects represent a regional network of more than 250 members involved with or interested in anti-trafficking activities, as well as national networks in each of the six participating countries.

An internet resource base
The project website provides contact details for organisations, as well as references, on-line material, and relevant links. Kvinnoforum and its collaborating partners are frequently invited to hold lectures, and to provide information and advice. The information gathered for the Resource Book was also presented on a project web-site, http://www.qweb.kvinnoforum.se/trafficking. The network services include keeping the members informed via e-mail about relevant news, reports, upcoming events, and activities.[10]

Conclusions and next steps

The human rights of trafficked women and girls are violated in many ways. Trafficking in women is a complex issue linked to development, poverty, health, and gender inequality that demands multifaceted responses. It is a contested problem, both in terms of its definition and in the attempts to formulate appropriate response strategies. The present paper has given an overview of trafficking, highlighting its complexity, the various actors, its causes and consequences, and the international statements condemning it.

Kvinnoforum and its partners aim to strengthen the network at national, regional, and global levels. The Kvinnoforum projects and activities have contributed to an enhanced awareness on trafficking in the Baltic Sea Region. There are now more anti-trafficking actors than there were in 1997, but there are not enough, and there is a need for more concrete activities to prevent trafficking and to support its victims. Finally, if we are to achieve long-term and sustainable change, anti-trafficking work must be framed in a gendered development perspective.

Carolina Johansson Wennerholm, Kvinnoforum, Tomtebogatan 42, 113 38 Stockholm, Sweden. Tel: + 468 56 22 88 00; fax: + 468 56 22 88 50
E-mail: carolina.wennerholm@kvinnoforum.se
http://www.kvinnoforum.se
http://www.qweb.kvinnoforum.se/trafficking

Notes

1 The overview part of this article is a shortened version of the background paper 'Trafficking in Women and

Children, an Overview' prepared for the UNFPA, 2001, and published with UNFPA's permission.

2 Protocol to Prevent, Suppress and Punish Trafficking in Persons, Especially Women and Children Supplementing the United Nations Convention against Transnational Organized Crime, Article 3: *'Trafficking in persons shall mean the recruitment, transportation, transfer, harbouring or receipt of persons, by means of the threat or use of force or other form of coercion, of abduction, of fraud, of deception, of the abuse of power or of a position of vulnerability or of the giving or receiving of payment or benefits to achieve the consent of a person having control over another person, for the purpose of exploitation. Exploitation shall include, at a minimum, the exploitation of the prostitution of others or other forms of sexual exploitation, forced labour or services, slavery or practices similar to slavery, servitude or the removal of organs;*
b) The consent of a victim in person to the intended exploitation set forth in subparagraphs (a) of this article shall be irrelevant where any of the means set forth in subparagraph (a) have been used;
c) The recruitment, transportation, transfer, harbouring or receipt of a child for the purpose of exploitation shall be considered "trafficking in persons", even if this does not involve any of the means set forth in sub paragraph (a) of this article;
d) Child shall mean any person under eighteen years of age.'

3 Reported by the Swedish NGO *Kvinna till Kvinna*, which has extensive experience of trafficking in the Balkan Region.

4 Reported by the Estonian NGO AIDSI TUGIKESKUS and the Latvian NGO Genders.

5 The networking project in the Baltic Region was initiated and run by Kvinnoforum in partnership with Monika, the Multicultural Women's Association in Finland, the PRO-centre in Denmark, the AIDS information and Support Centre AIDSI TUGIKESKUS in Estonia, the Latvian Gender Problem Centre, Latvia, and the Lithuanian Women's NGO PRAEITIES PEDOS, Lithuania.

6 The study was funded by the Swedish Minstry for Foreign Affairs.

7 Although trafficking occurs for domestic work, bounded labour in sweatshops, adoption, organ trafficking, marriage, and other purposes, the most common purpose is for the sex business. Thus the international debate related to prostitution has considerable impact on the general trafficking debate. The abolitionist view sees prostitution as an expression of violence and works to end it. At the other end of the spectrum, the Sex Workers Rights movement does not see prostitution *per se* as a problem, but rather the violence within the industry, and it aims to ensure that sex workers have legal rights as any other working group. Although both coalitions agree that trafficking must be addressed internationally, they do not co-operate, as their different ideological positions entail that discussions tend to end in opposing definitions (Strandberg 1999).

8 The project *'Crossing Borders Against Trafficking'* was carried out in 1998-9 with funding from the European Commission's Daphne Initiative and the Swedish Ministry for Foreign Affairs.

9 The project *'Training and Capacity Building against Trafficking in Women and Girls in the Baltic Sea Region'* was implemented during 1999-2000 with funding from the European Commission's Daphne Initiative and the Swedish Ministry for Foreign Affairs.

10 The trafficking work is thus integrated in Q Web, an internet-based global network for women's health and empowerment run by Kvinnoforum. See http://www.qweb.kvinnoforum.se

References

Coalition Against Trafficking in Women (CATW) (2001) 'Guide to the New UN Trafficking Protocol', North Amherst, MA: CATW

D'Cunha, J. (1992) 'Prostitution laws: ideological dimensions and enforcement practices', *Economic and Political Weekly* (Bombay), 24 April, cited in L.L. Lim (ed.) (1998)

Diakiti, F.S. (1999) 'Prostitution in Mali', in D. Hughes and C. Roche (eds) (1999)

EUROPOL (1999) 'Trafficking in Human Beings', General Situation Report, Open version, File-No: 2565-35 rev. 1, The Hague: EUROPOL

Foundation against Trafficking in Women (STV) (1996) 'International Report Project on Trafficking in Women: Latin America and Caribbean Region', Draft, August 31, Utrecht: STV

Gruenpeter Gold, L., N.B. Ami, S. Rosen, and N. Levenkron (2001) 'National NGOs Report to the Annual UN Commission on Human Rights: Evaluation of National Authorities Activities and Actual facts on the Trafficking in Persons for the Purpose of Prostitution in Israel', on behalf of Awareness Center and Hotline for Foreign Workers, March, Tel Aviv

Hughes, D. and J. Raymond (2001) *Sex Trafficking of Women in the United States, International and Domestic Trends*, Kingston, Rhode Island: CATW

Hughes, D. and C. Roche (eds) (1999) *Global Sexual Exploitation of Women and Girls, Speaking Out and Providing Services*, Kingston, Rhode Island: CATW

International Organisation for Migration (IOM) (2001) *Quarterly Bulletin* 23

Kvinnoforum (1999) *Trafficking in Women and Girls in the Baltic Sea Region, A Resource Book*, Stockholm: Kvinnoforum

Lim, L.L. (ed.) (1998) *The Sex Sector, The Economic and Social Bases of Prostitution in South-East Asia*, Geneva: ILO

Minnesota Advocates for Human Rights (MAHR) (2000) 'Trafficking in Women: Moldova and Ukraine', Minneapolis: MAHR

McDonald, L., B. Moore, and N. Timoshkina (2000) *Migrant Sex Workers from Eastern Europe and the Former Soviet Union: The Canadian Case*, Toronto: Centre for Applied Social Research, University of Toronto

O'Neill Richard, A. (1999) 'International Trafficking in Women to the United States: A Contemporary Manifestation of Slavery and Organized Crime', Washington, DC: Centre for the Study of Intelligence, http://www.cia.gov/csi/monograph/women/trafficking.pdf (last checked by author 5th May 2000)

Strandberg, N. (1999) 'What is trafficking and what can be done?', in Kvinnoforum (1999), http://www.qweb.kvinnoforum.se/papers/tic-whatistrafficking.html (last checked by author 11th January 2002)

Swedish Ministry for Foreign Affairs (2001) 'Trafficking in Women and Children in Asia and Europe, a Background Presentation of the Problems Involved and the Initiatives Taken', Stockholm: Swedish Ministry for Foreign Affairs

United Nations Office for Drug Control And Crime Prevention (UNODCCP) 'Trafficking in Person: the New Protocol', http://www.odccp.or/trafficking_protocol_backround.html (last checked by author 28th May 2001)

Who gets to choose?
Coercion, consent, and the UN Trafficking Protocol

Jo Doezema

This article explores the difficulties around using the notion of consent to define 'trafficking in women'. It does this through an examination of the recent negotiations around the UN Trafficking Protocol. 'Consent' was a highly contentious topic at the negotiations. One feminist lobby group argued that all prostitution, regardless of consent, should be considered trafficking. Another feminist lobby group insisted that coercion was a necessary element to any definition of trafficking. Government delegations tended to one or other of these positions. The final document attempts to compromise between these positions, with both lobby groups claiming victory for their position. This article looks at the arguments behind the interpretation of 'consent' in the negotiations, placing them in the historical context of early 20th century campaigns against white slavery. It suggests that views of female sexuality that see women as both more virtuous and more dangerous than men influence both historical and contemporary campaigns. It argues that current notions of 'consent', reflected in the ambiguity of the Protocol, are inadequate to serve as the basis for political strategies to protect the rights of sex workers and migrants.

In December 2000, over 80 countries signed the Protocol to Suppress, Prevent and Punish Trafficking in Persons, Especially Women and Children (The Trafficking Protocol) in Palermo, Italy. This event was the culmination of over two years of negotiations at the UN Centre for International Crime Prevention in Vienna. The Trafficking Protocol was the target of heavy feminist lobbying. These lobby efforts were split into two 'camps' espousing differing views on prostitution. One group, the Human Rights Caucus, viewed prostitution as legitimate labour. The other, represented by the Coalition Against Trafficking in Women (CATW), considered all forms of prostitution to be a violation of women's human rights.

Sex worker rights activists including myself were concerned about the impact of a new international trafficking instrument on the lives of sex workers. Historically, anti-trafficking measures have been used against sex workers, migrant sex workers, and immigrants. [1] Several activists from the Network of Sex Work Projects (NSWP) joined the Human Rights Caucus in their lobby efforts, in the hope of ensuring a result that would not damage sex workers' human rights. This paper reviews the arguments made by both lobby groups at the negotiations. It focuses in particular on how trafficking came to be defined, and the pivotal role played by the notion of 'consent'. It examines how 'consent' emerged as the international standard for determining 'trafficking in women', placing current debates in historical context. Finally, it assesses the potential for the Trafficking Protocol to be used to promote sex workers' and migrants' human rights.

Consent or coercion: negotiating the definition of trafficking

In Vienna, the differences between the lobby groups became most apparent during the most controversial part of the Protocol negotiations: deciding just how 'trafficking in persons' should be defined. CATW's lobby group argued that 'trafficking' should include all forms of recruitment and transportation for prostitution, regardless of whether any force or deception took place (CATW 1999). This is in line with their view of prostitution *per se* as a violation of women's human rights. The Human Rights Caucus, who supported the view of prostitution as work, argued that force or deception was a necessary condition in the definition of trafficking for sex work and for other types of labour. They also maintained that trafficking for prostitution should not be treated as a different category to other other types of labour. This was based on the recognition that men, women, and children are trafficked for a large variety of services, including sweatshop labour and agriculture (Human Rights Caucus 1999), as well as fear of the potentially repressive consequences of attemps to turn the Protocol into an anti-prostitution document.

These two positions ended up revolving around the notion of 'consent'. Several government delegations, backed by CATW's lobby group, argued that the definition of trafficking specifically had to include situations in which a person both consented to travel and consented to do sex work, even if no force or deception was involved. This position has at its root the assumption that a woman's consent to undertake sex work is meaningless. This definition of trafficking differed little from the proposed definition of trafficking in children: in this view, neither women or children can be said to 'consent' to travel for work in the sex industry.

Other governments opposed the attempts to define trafficking in women and children as essentially the same. Their position was endorsed by the Human Rights Caucus, who stated:

> *'Obviously, by definition, no one consents to abduction or forced labour, but an adult woman is able to consent to engage in an illicit activity (such as prostitution, where this is illegal or illegal for migrants). If no one is forcing her to engage in such an activity, then trafficking does not exist.... The Protocol should distinguish between adults, especially women, and children. It should also avoid adopting a patronizing stance that reduces women to the level of children, in the name of 'protecting' women. Such a stance historically has 'protected' women from the ability to exercise their rights.'* (Human Rights Caucus 1999, 5)

The argument that sex work is inherently a human rights violation, and thus cannot be consented to, is one that I disagree with. But it is not my intention in this paper to repeat the arguments for treating sex work as a legitimate profession.[2] Rather, I want to focus on the harmful political consequences of arguing that coercion (including deception) is not an essential part of any definition of trafficking. The argument that women cannot consent to commercial sexual interactions coincides all too easily with anti-feminist ideas about female sexuality, and particularly with that of the threat of women's sexual autonomy.[3] It also can be used to give what are basically anti-immigrant prejudices and policies a more palatable gloss, borrowing terms from human rights and feminist argumentation.

Consensual history

Historically, efforts to combat trafficking have ended up justifying repressive measures against prostitutes themselves in the name of 'protection' for women and children. Modern debates around the relationship of consent to 'trafficking in women' have a long history. At the beginning of the last century, there was a great public outcry against 'white slavery' in Europe and America. 'White slavery' referred to the abduction and transport of white women for prostitution.[4] In a manner similar to today's campaigns, the issue was covered widely in newspapers, a number of organisations were set up to combat it, and national and international legislation was adopted to stop the 'trade'. The international debates around 'white slavery' were highly concerned with the issue of consent. Many campaigners against the white slave trade saw all prostitutes as victims in need of rescue; others argued for the importance of distinguishing the 'willing' prostitute from the victimised white slave.

The distinction between 'white slaves' and willing prostitutes was maintained by campaigners of differing ideological bent. On the one hand were so-called 'purity' campaigners, who aimed to rid society of 'vice' and who focused in particular on youthful sexuality. For example, the US District Attorney Edwin W. Sims wrote in the preface to the influential 1910 tract, *Fighting the Traffic in Young Girls or War on the White Slave Trade*, 'The characteristic which distinguishes the white slave traffic from immorality [prostitution] in general is that the women who are the victims of the traffic are forced unwillingly to live an immoral life. The term "white slave" includes only those women and girls who are actually slaves.' (Sims 1910, 14) 'Purity' reformers' relationships with prostitutes themselves were ambiguous: while professing sympathy for the lost innocents sacrificed by white slavers, they were severe in their judgement of girls and women whose immodest behaviour led them into a life of shame.

On the other hand were the so-called 'regulationists', who believed that the 'necessary evil' of prostitution should be controlled by stringent state regulations. Dr. Parent-Duchatelet, whose 1836 study of French prostitutes was a model for regulationists, wrote: 'Prostitutes are as inevitable in a great conurbation as sewers, cesspits and refuse dumps. The conduct of the authorities should be the same with regard to each.' (in Roberts 1992, 223) Harnessing rational scientific arguments to moral disapproval, 'regulationists' argued that state regulation was the only way to control venereal disease. 'Innocent' women and girls needed protection from immorality; however, once fallen, it was society that needed protecting from the immoral woman. The best way to protect society, argued regulationists, was to register and medically control prostitutes.

Other campaigners, particularly women's rights activists, made little distinction between 'white slavery' and prostitution itself. These early feminists' attempts to break down the distinction between 'innocent' victims and 'immoral' prostitutes started with Josephine Butler's campaign against the regulation of prostitution through the Contagious Diseases Acts in Great Britain. Under these Acts, any woman who was suspected of prostitution could be detained by the police and forced to undergo an internal examination. Butler and other 'abolitionists' argued that men were responsible for prostitution, placing the blame for prostitution squarely on the shoulders of unbridled male lust. No women could be said to truly consent to prostitution: if a woman appeared 'willing', this was merely the result of the power that men held over her. By turning all prostitutes into victims, Butlerite feminists undercut the rationale for regulationist systems. When the Contagious Diseases Acts were repealed in 1886, Butler and her followers turned their attention to the fight against 'white slavery'. In the abolitionist vision, prostitution and white slavery would come to an end if laws targeted those who made money from prostitutes, rather than the prostitute herself. No woman would enter prostition of her own accord, they reasoned: with no one to lure or deceive her, woman's innate moral superiority would ensure her purity. In this, feminist abolitionists shared a view of women's sexuality that was common to all the various anti-white slavery campaigners. Women were considered sexually passive, which made them more 'virtuous' than men, but, paradoxically, once that virtue was 'lost' through illicit sexual behaviour, women's sexual nature became dangerous. Consequently, calls for the need to protect women's purity alternated with attempts to reform and discipline prostitutes.

Feminist abolitionists displayed a curious mixture of a progressive refusal to condemn prostitutes, and a moralistic, middle-class urge to protect the virtue of young, working class, and immigrant women. This ambiguity is clearly illustrated in the work of the notable US feminist campaigner, Jane Addams. In her book on 'white slavery', *A New Conscience and an Ancient Evil*, Addams argues forcefully against police harassment of prostitutes and for improved wages for working women. While she relates with heart-rending pathos the stories of poor girls whose only hope of feeding their families is by giving in to the blandishments of 'white slavers', she is scornful and dismissive of those girls who would contemplate selling their virtue in slightly less desperate circumstances:

> *'Although economic pressure as a reason for entering an illicit life has thus been brought out in court by the evidence in a surprising number of cases, there is no doubt that it is often exaggerated; a girl always prefers to think that economic pressure is the reason for her downfall, even when the immediate causes have been her love of pleasure, her desire for finery, or the influence of evil companions.'* (Addams 1912, 60)

According to Addams, these moral failings made young working-class and immigrant girls 'easy prey' for white slavers. Certainly, belief in these girls' innate moral weakness made them the ideal target of the reforming impulses of middle-class feminists.

The consequences of denying consent

The first international agreement against 'white slavery' was drafted in 1902 in Paris and signed in 1904 by 16 states. Largely due to the input of regulationist countries such as France, the International Agreement for the Suppression of the White Slave Trade did not equate 'white slavery' with 'prostitution'. The agreement only addresses the fraudulent or abusive recruitment of women for prostitution in another country. In 1910, a new agreement broadened the scope of the crime to include recruitment for prostitution within national boundaries. Both of these conventions were limited to the traffic in 'unwilling' women, and covered only recruitment, not conditions in prostitution workplaces.[5] It was not until 1933 that an international agreement was drafted that reflected the abolitionist position. The International Convention for the Suppression of the Traffic in Women condemned all recruitment for prostitution in another country. It obliges states to punish 'any person who, in order to gratify the passions of another person, procures, entices or leads away, *even with her consent*, a woman or a girl of full age for immoral purposes to be carried out in another country' (in Wijers and Lap-Chew 1997, emphasis added).[6]

If it took until 1933 for the abolitionist position to become encoded in international law, abolitionist influence on national legislation in several countries was much more marked. Throughout Europe and in the USA, anti-white slavery activists were successful in their campaigns for abolitionist laws aimed at protecting prostitutes from 'white slavers', 'pimps', and 'profiteers'. These new laws neither ended prostitution nor improved prostitutes' working conditions: rather, these laws were used against prostitutes themselves. Thrown out of brothels and red-light districts, prostitutes were forced into illegality, and arrests of prostitutes actually increased. Prostitutes' husbands and boyfriends were targeted as pimps, especially if they were black or 'foreign'. In a famous case in the USA, the 1910 Mann Act (The White Slave Traffic Act) was used to punish Jack Johnson, a black boxer, for his marriage to a white woman.[7] In Britain, the Criminal Law Amendment Bill of 1921 (The White Slave Act) was used against prostitutes and working class women (Walkowitz 1980). Greece fought 'white slavery' by passing legislation in 1912 forbidding women under 21 to travel abroad without a special permit (Bristow 1977, 178).

Ambiguous standards

The legacy of abolitionism is still being felt today. In international law, the abolitionist standards of the 1933 Convention were reiterated in the 1949 UN Convention for the Suppression of the Traffic in Persons and the Exploitation of the Prostitution of Others. In this agreement, prostitution is considered incompatible with the dignity of the person. Until the adoption of the Trafficking Protocol, this was the only international document to deal comprehensively with trafficking and prostitution. Though signed by few countries, the 1949 Convention served as a model for much domestic legislation. In a large number of countries, abolitionist laws are still on the books: preventing prostitutes working together (lest one be arrested for pimping), blocking prostitutes' attempts at union-forming (considered as unlawful 'promotion of prostitution'), and barring them from legal redress in cases of violations of their labour, civil, and human rights.

If there is one lesson that we can learn from history, it is that increased state power to repress prostitution ends up being used against prostitutes themselves. Has history repeated itself in the Trafficking Protocol? The answer is not yet clear, but the Protocol has the potential to be used for repressive as well as for emancipatory ends. On the one hand, the final definition of trafficking in the Protocol can be considered a victory for those who argue that the only way to protect sex workers' rights is to recognise prostitution as a legitimate profession. The use of force or coercion is included as an essential element of trafficking in the definition. This is a significant departure from the abolitionist stance of the 1949 Convention, and leaves states free to recognise sex work as labour and regulate it according to labour standards. On the other hand, while the Protocol makes an implicit distinction between 'coerced' and 'non-coerced' migration for prostitution, it offers very little in terms of human rights protections for trafficking victims, and nothing at all for (migrant) sex workers who were not coerced. If the Protocol leaves the way free for governments to treat sex work as labour, it also in no way prevents governments from persecuting, criminalising, and denying equal protection of the law to sex workers in the name of fighting 'trafficking'.

Conclusion: beyond 'trafficking'?

Despite the potential of the Trafficking Protocol to be used to protect (migrant) sex workers' human rights, recent government actions seem to indicate that the repressive potential of the Protocol will prevail. In a number of countries, anti-trafficking measures have led to restrictions on movement and migration for women, increased surveillance of sex workers, and increased deportation of migrant sex workers. This point was made forcefully by Radhika Coomaraswamy, the UN Special Rapporteur on Violence Against Women, its Causes and Consequences, at a recent conference.[8] Arguing that 'trafficking' and 'prostitution' should not be linked, she described how many Asian governments were responding to trafficking fears by legislating to restrict women's freedom of movement. Deportations of sex workers are commonplace. One recent example is in the UK, where the police raided London brothels, and migrant sex workers were deported. In the Netherlands, trafficking fears have led to a law which requires all sex workers to carry identification papers – the only occupational group for whom this is required.

The lessons from history about the repressive consequences of anti-trafficking laws have led some activists to search for a new way to conceptualise migration and prostitution. The contours of a framework to replace that of trafficking have begun to emerge, sketched out in discussions, demands, and demonstrations from Delhi to Detroit by sex workers and those who support their agenda. This new framework would reject both the neo-abolitionist position that would deny women the ability to consent to prostitution, and a neo-regulationist perspective that condemns 'forced' prostitution but offers nothing in the way of rights for the 'guilty', 'voluntary' prostitutes. This new framework would incorporate elements of labour rights, insisting that sex workers be treated as legitimate workers, rather than as moral reprobates. It would challenge the mentality that demands that women bear responsibility for the moral guardianship of society. It would recognise that gender relations in the sex industry are not a simple matter of oppressed women and oppressive men, but that men, women, and transgenders take up varying positions and have varying amounts of power as clients, sex workers, and associates. It would grant Third World women the same degree of self-awareness, autonomy, and agency that is taken as self-evident for Western women. Most importantly, this new framework may be able to move beyond the legacy of repression clinging to the trafficking framework because it will be developed by sex workers themselves.

Jo Doezema is studying for her doctoral thesis at the Institute of Development Studies, University of Sussex, Brighton BN1 9RE, UK. Tel: +44 (0)1273 606 261 ext. 4153

Notes

1. See NSWP 1999.
2. For discussions of prostitution as sex work, see P. Alexander and F. Delacoste (eds) (1987); G. Pheterson (ed.) (1989); W. Chapkis (1997); Bindman and Doezema (1997); J. Nagle (ed.) (1997); Doezema (1998).
3. See Doezema 2001.
4. Historians who have studied the period have almost all come to the conclusion that there were actually very few cases of white slavery (see Connelly 1980; Grittner 1990; Guy 1991). There was, however, a large increase in migration from Southern and Eastern Europe to the USA and Latin America. Many of those who migrated were prostitutes, who carried on working in their new lands. While these women certainly enjoyed no 'rights' as we would term them, neither is there evidence that they were the sex slaves of popular myth. Historians such as Grittner (1990) argue that 'white slavery' was a 'cultural myth': a collective belief that simplifies reality and that expresses deep societal fears and anxieties. 'White slavery' as a cultural myth stood for fears about immigration, racist anxieties, fears about industrialisation and urbanisation, and

about women's increasing independence. For an examination of 'trafficking in women' as a cultural myth, see Doezema (2000).

5 See Wijers and Lap-Chew (1997) and Haveman (1998).

6 The abolitionist position continued to dominate international law until the 1980s, when a number of agreements began to recognise a distinction between 'voluntary' and 'forced' prostitution. See Doezema (1998).

7 See Roberts (1986) for an account of the Jackson case.

8 'Prostitution, Trafficking and the Global Sex Trade in Women', NYU Law School, March 2, 2001

References

Addams, J. (1912) *A New Conscience and an Ancient Evil*, New York: Macmillan

Alexander, P. and F. Delacoste (eds) (1987) *Sex Work: Writings by Women in the Sex Industry*, Pittsburgh: Cleis Press

Bindman, J. and J. Doezema (1997) *Redefining Prostitution as Sex Work on the International Agenda*, London: Anti-Slavery International and the Network of Sex Work Projects

Bristow, E.J. (1977) *Vice and Vigilance: Purity Movements in Britain since 1700*, Dublin: Gill and Macmillan

Coalition Against Trafficking in Women (CATW) (1999) 'Prostitutes Work, But Do They Consent?', http://www.uri.edu/artsci/wms/hughes/catw (last checked by author May 2001)

Chapkis, W. (1997) *Live Sex Acts: Women Performing Erotic Labor*, New York and London: Routledge

Connelly, M.T. (1980) *The Response to Prostitution in the Progressive Era*, Chapel Hill: University of North Carolina Press

Doezema, J. (1998) 'Forced to choose: beyond the free v. forced prostitution dichotomy', in K. Kempadoo and J. Doezema (eds) *Global Sex Workers: Rights, Resistance and Redefinition*, New York and London: Routledge

Doezema, J. (2000) 'Loose women or lost women? The re-emergence of the myth of white slavery in contemporary discourses of trafficking in women', *Gender Issues* 18(1): 38-54

Doezema, J. (2001) 'Ouch! Western feminists' "wounded attachment" to the "third-world prostitute"', *Feminist Review* 67: 16-38

Grittner, F.K. (1990) *White Slavery: Myth, Ideology and American Law*, New York and London: Garland

Guy, D.J. (1991) *Sex and Danger in Buenos Aires: Prostitution, Family and Nation in Argentina*, Lincoln and London: University of Nebraska Press

Haveman, R. (1998) *Voorwaarden voor Strafbaarstelling van Vrouwenhandel*, Doctoral Thesis, University of Utrecht, Utrecht: Gouda Quint

Human Rights Caucus (1999) 'Recommendations and Commentary on the Draft Protocol to Combat International Trafficking in Women and Children Supplementary to the Draft Convention on Transnational Organised Crime', http://www.hrlawgroup.org/site/programs/traffic (last checked by author December 2001)

Nagle, J. (ed.) (1998) *Whores and Other Feminists*, New York and London: Routledge

Network of Sex Work Projects (1999) 'Commentary On The Draft Protocol To Combat International Trafficking In Women And Children Supplementary To The Draft Convention On Transnational Organized Crime' (A/AC.254/4/add.3), http://www.walnet.org/nswp (last checked by author December 2001)

Pheterson, G. (ed.) (1989) *A Vindication of the Rights of Whores*, Seattle: Seal Press

Roberts, N. (1992) *Whores in History: Prostitution in Western Society*, London: HarperCollins

Roberts, R. (1986) *Papa Jack: Jack Johnson and the Era of White Hopes*, London: Robson

Walkowitz, J. (1980) *Prostitution and Victorian Society: Women, Class and the State*, Cambridge: CUP

Wijers, M. and L. Lap-Chew (1997) *Trafficking in Women, Forced Labour and Slavery-Like Practices in Marriage, Domestic Labour and Prostitution*: Utrecht and Bangkok: Foundation Against Trafficking in Women (STV) and Global Alliance Against Trafficking in Women (GAATW)

Human rights or wrongs?

The struggle for a rights-based response to trafficking in human beings

Ann D. Jordan

A unique opportunity for non-governmental organisations (NGOs) and advocates to contribute to the development of a human rights-based response to the trafficking of human beings now exists. Many governments have signed a new international treaty on trafficking and are in the process of adopting domestic anti-trafficking laws. However, as explained in this article, most government officials are uninformed about the causes and consequences of trafficking, and the appropriate rights-based legal responses. NGOs can bring their expertise and a human rights framework to the debate by working with government officials to draft and implement new trafficking laws and policies. This article offers a brief introduction and guidance to some of the challenges that NGOs will face in their advocacy work

Trafficking of human beings is the movement of persons within or across borders by any means (such as force or fraud) into forced labour, slavery, or servitude. It has always existed; however, its phenomenal growth in the last quarter of the 20th century has caused alarm around the world. It is now a multi-billion dollar industry run by individuals and small and large organised criminal networks. Although precise statistics do not exist, anecdotal evidence and studies indicate that hundreds of thousands – if not several millions – of people are trafficked worldwide annually. Experts agree that a disproportionate number of trafficked persons are women and girls.

This phenomenal growth has resulted from the simultaneous existence of a number of push, pull, and facilitating factors. The push factors include the increase in civil wars since the fall of Soviet Union, the collapse of the Chinese socialist system, environmental damage, natural disasters, violence in the family, and uneven economic growth. Women's unequal status in societies worldwide means that the burden of poverty and the direct and indirect consequences of violence impact disproportionately on women. This has resulted in an out-migration of women from poor countries and conflict areas, larger than any before. Many of these women are particularly vulnerable, and end up being trafficked.

At the same time, the absolute or relative prosperity and peace in industrialised and newly industrialising countries act as 'pull' factors in international migration. Growing economies create increased demand for imported labour as citizens increasingly refuse to take low-paying jobs. Young women are in particular demand because they are considered to be more compliant and detail-oriented, and less likely to rebel against the conditions of forced labour. Some young women are pulled into migration by the prospect of marriage and a better life abroad. Some of these marriages are arranged by unscrupulous brokers, with women being trafficked into servile marriages.

These push and pull factors lay the causal foundation for trafficking. In additon, there exist a number of facilitating factors that make trafficking possible. Growth in the industrialised economies has been accompanied by a quantum leap in low-cost transportation and communication technologies. Many traffickers with legal status abroad fly to their countries of origin to find new recruits for forced labour. They use modern technologies to transport their victims with little risk of detection.

Corruption plays a crucial facilitating role. As the socialist systems and economies of the former Soviet Union and elsewhere collapsed, some civil servant salaries fell below the poverty level. As a result, criminal activities in many countries are organised by, or with the co-operation of, officials. Corruption is so extensive in some countries that victims who escape and report to the police risk being sent *back* to the traffickers. Under these conditions, traffickers no longer need to build walls or put bars on windows.

Xenophobic, tightly controlled immigration laws in destination countries also facilitate trafficking (Morrison 2000). Countries of destination grant visas for highly-skilled workers but not for unskilled workers despite the existence of millions of low-skilled jobs. The gap between strict immigration policies and the need for migrant labour provides a perfect environment for trafficking. Trafficking will probably increase, for example, in Europe, where the demand for labour will continue to grow as birth rates continue to decline.

Weaknesses of domestic legal responses

The common thread running through government responses to trafficking is the prevalence of inappropriate or inadequate laws and policies. Governments either provide some protections to some victims,[1] or no protections at all.[2] A partial exception to this bleak picture is the recent US legislation, which covers all forms of trafficking and all persons.[3] The new law is not perfect – some trafficked persons will not be protected – but it is better than most other countries' laws at present.

There are four primary reasons for inappropriate or inadequate responses to trafficking.

1. Denial of the problem

Many governments are unwilling to acknowledge the existence of trafficking, or only recognise trafficking of women into forced prostitution. Even when presented with incontrovertible evidence of extensive trafficking of all forms, many governments still refuse to acknowledge that trafficking is a problem.

A number of means are necessary to force governments to act. Research has the potential to reveal the scope of the problem, if not the exact numbers of people involved. Research should cover all forms of trafficking, e.g., trafficking of women into forced prostitution, forced marriages, and forced domestic work, and of men, women, and children into forced labour or slavery in factories, fields, streets, and homes. Undercover videos, high-profile media campaigns, and international pressure are important tools that have been successful in many countries.

2. Objectifying victims and failing to consider their human rights

Governments consistently fail to consider the crime from the perspective of the trafficked person and are particularly inept at understanding the problem from the perspective of trafficked women. They view trafficking as a problem of organised crime, migration, and/or prostitution, rather than as a human rights abuse. Thus, advocates bear the burden of educating authorities on the rights and needs of trafficked persons. A particularly difficult aspect of this work involves demonstrating to authorities that women who are trafficked into forced prostitution, forced domestic work, and other forms of forced labour should not be deprived of their rights on the grounds that they are undocumented migrants who 'knew' what to expect and so deserved what they 'got'.

Even governments and NGOs that are sincerely concerned about the situation of trafficked women often treat the women as vulnerable and passive objects who are incapable of making reasoned judgments and, consequently, need to be rescued and 'rehabilitated'. The reality often stands in stark contrast. Trafficked women, and men, are likely to be strong, risk-taking individuals who have made rational choices and exercised their own agency in deciding to migrate. Unfortunately, they become victims of traffickers. They often have compelling reasons for leaving home, and those reasons remain once they are freed. From the trafficked person's perspective, their need to feed a family or send siblings to school may be stronger than their desire to see their traffickers brought to justice.

The human rights framework shifts the focus away from seeing trafficked persons as objects towards understanding them as people bearing human rights. It also overcomes anti-immigrant bias, misogyny, and contempt towards those trafficked persons who are also voluntary sex workers. The human rights framework dictates an empowerment approach to assisting trafficked persons in retaking control over their lives and in ensuring that women are treated as adults, not children.

3. Conflation of trafficking with undocumented migration

Governments consistently conflate trafficking with undocumented migration. They argue that undocumented migrants and trafficked persons should be treated in the same way in order to discourage future undocumented migration. They adopt a two-tiered approach to human rights wherein only citizens have rights, despite the fact that international human rights law does not predicate the majority of rights upon citizenship. This approach allows governments to treat trafficked persons and undocumented migrants in the same manner – to deport them immediately. As a result, traffickers are not prosecuted; instead the victims may be prosecuted for immigration and labour violations. Some governments only prosecute trafficking into forced prostitution, and may deport trafficked persons when their testimony is no longer needed.

Advocates are constantly forced to educate officials on the difference between trafficking and smuggling. Their work can be supported by gathering stories about the negative consequences of failing to distinguish between the two, for example, about returnees who are harmed or retrafficked as a result of summary deportations. However, unless underlying causes such as unemployment, political instability, gender discrimination in education, employment, the family, and the political arena, and unrealistic immigration laws, are addressed, undocumented labour migration will continue to increase, as will trafficking of women.

4. Improper definition of the crime

Most governments (and some NGOs) only address the trafficking of women (and children) into forced prostitution. This is especially a problem in Western Europe, where other forms of trafficking are ignored completely. This approach privileges one gender-specific group of victims. It ensures that women, men, and children who are trafficked into other forms of forced labour, slavery, or servitude, and young men who are trafficked into forced prostitution are not protected, and that their traffickers are not prosecuted.

The tendency to objectify trafficked persons is doubly problematic when the focus is only on women (and children) who are trafficked into forced prostitution. This gendered focus and conflation of trafficking with forced prostitution is especially problematic in Western Europe, where governments and NGOs ignore other forms of trafficking as well as the trafficking of men. Women trafficked into forced prostitution are treated as 'madonnas' (innocent, vulnerable) who need assistance and support or as 'whores' (conniving, tainted) who need redemption and rehabilitation. Governments and some NGOs are eager to help 'madonna' victims but not 'whore' victims. Objectification can also lead to laws and policies depriving young women of their right to leave their countries of citizenship (often with the support of local NGOs) by withholding passports or stopping women at the border. A human rights approach would lessen the potential for such discriminatory responses.

Another negative consequence of conflating trafficking with prostitution is the development of abolitionist proposals to criminalise prostitution and clients (but not the sex workers). Abolitionists believe that, by magically prohibiting prostitution, all forced prostitution and trafficking into prostitution will disappear.[4] On the contrary, criminalising prostitution and clients simply gives more power to criminals. It forces independent sex workers into the hands of third parties who offer protection from arrest and police abuse. Once the industry is pushed underground, organised crime takes over, and trafficking into forced prostitution increases.

For example, trafficking in Sweden has increased since January 1999, when Sweden began criminalising clients of sex workers. A National Criminal Police Report found that, 'Sweden's sex trade was in danger of becoming more violent in the future, as the law in fact encouraged more women to be brought in from overseas.' It concluded that the new law is protecting the criminals who now control the industry (Goldsmith 1999). Conversations by the author with sex workers in Sweden confirm that the new law has forced independent Swedish and other European sex workers underground. It has also led to increased trafficking of non-Western European women into forced prostitution.

In sum, current legal responses are discriminatory, and violate the rights of some or all trafficked persons. They also fail to increase prosecutions or reduce undocumented migration because they fail to observe the rights of trafficked persons, or to treat them with dignity and respect.

The lost opportunity for an international human rights framework

Until recently, no international legal framework existed specifically to address all forms of trafficking,[5] even though all of the human rights violations that occur in trafficking are covered by existing human rights instruments.[6] An historic opportunity to incorporate those rights into a new international treaty recently occurred when the United Nations adopted the Protocol to Prevent, Suppress, and Punish Trafficking in Persons, especially Women and Children (United Nations 2000b, c). The complete Protocol (United Nations 2000d) consists of three documents: the Protocol itself, relevant provisions of the new Convention Against Transnational Organized Crime (United Nations 2000a), and the Interpretative Notes to the Protocol (United Nations 2000e).

The Protocol was created at the UN Commission on Crime Prevention and Criminal Justice in Vienna rather than at one of the human rights bodies located in Geneva. The NGO community was represented by the Human Rights Caucus,[7] which had two goals: to ensure that the first international definition of trafficking recognises that women, men, and children are trafficked into forced labour, slavery, and servitude; and to incorporate a human rights framework into the final document.

The Human Rights Caucus was successful in achieving the first goal.

The first international definition of trafficking reads:

'"Trafficking in persons" shall mean the recruitment, transportation, transfer, harbouring or receipt of persons, by means of the threat or use of force or other forms of coercion, of abduction, of fraud, of deception, of the abuse of power or of a position of vulnerability or of the giving or receiving of payments or benefits to achieve the consent of a person having control over another person, for the purpose of exploitation. Exploitation shall include, at a minimum, the exploitation of the prostitution of others or other forms of sexual exploitation, forced labour or services, slavery or practices similar to slavery, servitude or the removal or organs.'

Slavery, forced labour or services, and servitude are all defined in other international instruments[8] and cover all forms of trafficking. The terms 'exploitation of the prostitution of others' and 'sexual exploitation' are not defined in the Protocol or anywhere else in international law. They are undefined and included in the definition as a means to end an unnecessary yearlong debate over whether or not voluntary adult prostitution should be defined as trafficking. Delegates were unable to reach any agreement on this point and so finally compromised on the last day of the negotiations by leaving the terms undefined. This ensures that governments will be able to sign the Protocol, despite their different laws on sex work.

The compromise is explained in the Interpretative Notes (*Travaux préparatoires*) to the Protocol:

'The Travaux préparatoires *should indicate that the Protocol addresses the exploitation of the prostitution of others and other forms of sexual exploitation only in the context of trafficking in persons. The terms "exploitation of the prostitution of others" or "other forms of sexual exploitation" are not defined in the Protocol, which is therefore without prejudice to how States Parties address prostitution in their respective domestic laws.'* (United Nations 2000e)

Thus, the compromise recognises the difference between forced (or involuntary) and voluntary adult participation in sex work. Governments can choose to define the terms in any way they choose. However, there is no reason to include the two undefined terms in domestic legislation because they only add unnecessary confusion. Additionally, all possible forms of trafficking are included in the terms 'forced labour or services, slavery and servitude'. *Involuntary* sex work (like other forms of involuntary or forced labour) is covered by the term 'forced labour or services'. Furthermore, *voluntary* migrant sex work (like other forms of voluntary migrant labour) is covered by the Smuggling Protocol.

Countries that decide, nonetheless, to include those two terms in their domestic laws will have to define them. Every element of a criminal prohibition must be clearly stated so that the public is given notice about the prohibited activity, and judges and juries will be able to determine guilt or innocence. Undefined crimes violate international human rights norms and most (or all) of the world's constitutions.

The Human Rights Caucus was less successful in achieving its second goal. Delegates insisted that the Protocol is a 'law enforcement' instrument, and that protections must be linked to law enforcement goals, such as witness protection. Despite the best efforts of the Human Rights Caucus and a few delegations to raise the human rights issues, there was no time to discuss protections because so much time was wasted on the yearlong debate over prostitution.

The final Protocol, then, is primarily a law enforcement tool. Governments 'shall adopt' laws to criminalise trafficking, share information, and extradite suspected traffickers. They only 'shall consider' and 'shall endeavour' to provide assistance and protections. The Protocol perpetuates the two-tiered approach to human rights.

A unique opportunity to bring human rights to the foreground of the international legal response to trafficking was thus lost and another similar opportunity is highly unlikely. Consequently, the focus now shifts to the national level, and the burden of advocating for rights-protective national legislation and policies shifts to domestic NGOs.

Opportunity and challenge for rights-protective domestic legislative responses

NGOs can seize this unique opportunity. Never again will so many countries be focusing at one time on trafficking legislation and policies. All countries that ratify the Protocol are obliged to adopt legislation implementing the Protocol and relevant provisions of the Convention. Many countries are already drafting new laws and most have little understanding of the problem, or what appropriate responses should be. NGOs can provide much-needed insights on the gender-based causes and consequences of trafficking and appropriate legal responses.

However, most NGOs are unfamiliar with the Protocol and need training, education, and advocacy materials, and access to networks with expertise. NGOs can study the new Protocol, including the Convention and the Interpretative Notes (United Nation 2000d), and the Human Rights Standards for the Treatment of Trafficked Persons (GAATW *et al.* 1999). The Human Rights Standards were developed by organisations worldwide that work with, or advocate on behalf of, trafficked persons. They are based upon existing international human rights norms. The Human Rights Standards document contains specific recommendations on measures that governments should adopt in order to avoid re-victimising trafficked persons. The main goal of advocacy would be to ensure that all of the Protocol provisions (including relevant sections of the Convention) and all of the protections called for in the Human Rights Standards are adopted into domestic law.

Advocates can also refer to legislation in other countries, but with a highly critical eye, as bad practices unfortunately far outnumber good practices. Paternalistic attitudes or anti-immigration policies are the norm.

Advocates might consider encouraging their governments to incorporate the following measures, at a minimum, into the trafficking law and policy responses:

Equality

Trafficking laws must be interpreted and applied in a non-discriminatory manner to all persons,[9] which means that women and men should have equal access to justice, protections, assistance, and immigration relief in origin and destination countries. Governments must address the root causes of trafficking, particularly discriminatory laws and practices that result in higher illiteracy for girls, higher unemployment for women, denial of women's rights to choose a spouse and plan a future, and lack of protection of women and children from violence in the home and in society.

Access to justice

The Protocol obliges governments to criminalise trafficking[10] and corruption, and vigorously to investigate and prosecute officials at all levels.[11]

Governments must also ensure that trafficked persons have the right to sue their traffickers for the harm they have suffered. Governments must 'ensure' that trafficked persons have 'the possibility of obtaining compensation for damage suffered'.[12] The Convention requires governments to confiscate the assets of the traffickers,[13] but is silent about how to use the assets. Delegates to the negotiations refused to adopt a Human Rights Caucus proposal to use confiscated assets, first, to pay compensation and reintegration costs to trafficked persons;[14] second, to pay for services to trafficked persons in origin and destination countries; and, third, to fund anti-trafficking programs in origin and destination countries.

Trafficked persons must not be prosecuted for undocumented entry or unauthorised work. Specific language may be necessary to ensure that trafficked persons are never prosecuted for prostitution-related offenses, even if prostitution is prohibited.

Protection of trafficked persons

Governments have an obligation to ensure the security of every person.[15] The Protocol and the Convention call upon governments to protect the identity and privacy of trafficked persons, to keep legal proceedings confidential,[16] and to protect witnesses.[17] Domestic law should incorporate these protections and also provide protections for relatives who are similarly threatened. Government should also protect trafficked persons who are not witnesses but who are threatened.

Immigration law

Governments must reform their immigration laws to allow people to migrate legally to meet the domestic demand for labour. Research and scholarship are needed to document the link in order to gather support for appropriate immigration law reform.

Immigration laws should not be used to punish trafficked persons. Trafficked persons must not be subjected to the same treatment as undocumented migrants. They should be allowed to remain for a reasonable period of time so that they can regain control over their lives. During this period, they should be able to contact a doctor and a lawyer, analyse legal options, and contact family members and friends at home to determine whether it is safe to return.

The Protocol's immigration provisions are weak and allow governments to choose whether or not to provide temporary residence.[18] However, governments should not summarily deport trafficked persons who, by definition, have been subjected to horrific abuse. Summary deportation denies trafficked persons access to justice, and may place them at risk of retaliation back home.

The law should also provide for longer stays for witnesses in criminal prosecutions and for trafficked persons who file civil claims against the traffickers. It should grant permanent residence if returning home is unsafe or reintegration into the home community would be extremely difficult.[19] The Protocol language is very weak on this point but it does encourage governments to offer permanent residence 'in appropriate cases'.[20] Provisions should also be adopted to permit family members to join trafficked persons, if necessary.[21]

Governments should take steps to prevent trafficking of migrant domestic workers and foreign fiancées. For example, women should be given information about their legal rights in the destination country. A mechanism might be developed to ensure that, upon arrival, foreign domestic workers and fiancées are placed in contact with supporting NGOs.

Additionally, individuals who facilitate the importation of domestic workers and fiancées should be required, under criminal sanctions, to disclose fully to women the background of their potential employer or husband, including providing women with official government reports on any criminal background, financial situation, and present and prior marriages, particularly the existence of any prior marriages to immigrant women.

Lastly, governments must adopt and enforce a policy ensuring that all persons with diplomatic immunity who traffic domestic workers are expelled from the country. At present, trafficking diplomats are totally exempt from prosecution, are not prevented from bringing in more domestic workers, and are rarely expelled (Connor 2001).

Provision of basic services

Governments at the Protocol negotiations refused to accept an obligation to provide services to trafficked persons despite the existence of human rights principles that 'recognize the right of everyone [including non-citizens] to an adequate standard of living..., including adequate food, clothing, and housing', 'the fundamental right of everyone to be free from hunger',[22] and the obligation to create 'the conditions which would assure all medical service and medical attention in the event of sickness.'[23] Some delegates objected in principle and other raised financial concerns.

Delegates from poorer countries pointed out that their governments cannot afford to pay for services for their own citizens, let alone for immigrants. A Human Rights Caucus proposal to exempt poor countries from providing services until they are financially capable of doing so was not adopted.[24]

If governments fail to provide any services, then NGOs will face the entire burden of providing services and seeking financial support from the government and other sources. The following services, which could be funded – at least in part – from confiscated assets, should be provided or funded by the government:

- basic medical and mental health care;
- shelter that is not a form of prison or detention;
- protection from the traffickers;
- access to information on legal rights and to attorneys or advocates;
- financial or other assistance, for example, for food, clothing, and telephone calls home;
- a means to return home safely.

Conclusion

Trafficking in human beings is high on the international agenda at present. Despite this, NGOs face significant difficulties in overcoming official reluctance to accept responsibility for the protection of the rights of trafficked persons. However, by working together to bring their voices and the voices of trafficked persons to the highest national and international levels, they can make a difference. They will ensure that this unique opportunity to impact on the lives of hundreds of thousands, perhaps millions, of people worldwide is not lost.

Ann Jordan is Director of the Initiative Against Trafficking in Persons at the International Human Rights Law Group, 1200 18th Street NW, Washington, DC 20008, USA.
Tel: +1 202 822-4600, ext. 27;
fax: +1 202 822 4606;
http://www.hrlawgroup.org/initiatives/trafficking_persons/

Notes

1 For example, anti-trafficking laws in Belgium, the Netherlands, and Italy only cover trafficking into forced sex work.

2 The majority of countries do not have laws criminalising trafficking into forced labour, slavery, or servitude.

3 Victims of Trafficking and Violence Protection Act of 2000 (HR 3244)

4 An analogous approach would be to criminalise all domestic or factory work because some people are trafficked into those forms of labour.

5 The Convention for the Suppression of the Traffic in Persons and of the Exploitation of the Prostitution of Others

is an anti-sex work instrument. It has had a negative impact on women because it has forced the sex industry underground and pushed women into the hands of organised criminals. It does not address trafficking into forced labour, slavery, and servitude, hence the need for a new international instrument.

6 For example, in the Slavery Convention, the Supplemental Convention on the Abolition of Slavery, the Slave Trade, and Institutions and Practices Similar to Slavery; and the International Labour Organisation Convention no. 29 Concerning Forced Labor.

7 The Human Rights Caucus members are: the International Human Rights Law Group, Foundation Against Trafficking in Women, Global Alliance Against Traffic in Women, Asian Women's Human Rights Council, La Strada, Ban-Ying, Fundación Esperanza, Foundation for Women, KOK-NGO Network Against Trafficking in Women, Women's Consortium of Nigeria, and Women, Law and Development in Africa (Nigeria).

8 Slavery Convention, art. 1: 'Slavery is the status or condition of a person over whom any or all of the powers attaching to the right of ownership are exercised.' ILO Convention no. 19 Concerning Forced Labor, art. 2: 'Forced or compulsory labor [is] all work or service which is exacted from any person under the menace of any penalty and for which the said person has not offered himself voluntarily.' Section I of the Supplementary Convention on the Abolition of Slavery describes some types of 'servitude'.

9 Protocol, article 14.2

10 Protocol, article 5

11 Convention on Transnational Organized Crime, article 8

12 Protocol, section 6.6

13 Convention on Transnational Organized Crime, article 12

14 Some countries pay compensation and other claims out of confiscated assets. Others have said they will not do so.

15 International Covenant on Civil and Political Rights, article 9.1

16 Protocol, article 6.1

17 Convention on Transnational Organized Crime, article 24

18 Protocol, article 7

19 For example, US and Belgium laws make permanent residence available under certain circumstances.

20 Protocol, article 8

21 For example, US law authorises visas for family members under certain circumstances

22 International Covenant on Economic, Social and Cultural Rights, articles 11.2 and 11.3 (United Nations 2002)

23 International Covenant on Economic, Social and Cultural Rights, article. 12.2(d) (United Nations 2002)

24 Protocol, article 6.3

References

Connor, J. (2001) 'Domestic Slavery', a Report prepared for the Council of Europe Committee on Equal Opportunities for Women and Men, Document 9102, 17 May 2001, http://stars.coe.fr/doc/doc01/EDOC9102.htm (last checked by author February 2002)

Global Alliance Against Trafficking in Women (GAATW) *et al.* (1999) 'The Human Rights Standards for the Treatment of Trafficked Persons', http://www.hrlawgroup.org/initiatives/trafficking_persons/ and http://wagner.inet.co.th/org/gaatw/index.html (last checked by author February 2002)

Goldsmith, B. (1999) 'Swedish law fails to curb prostitution', Stockholm: Reuters Stockholm, 7 May

Morrison, J. (2000) 'The Trafficking and Smuggling of Refugees: The End Game in European Asylum Policy?', http://www.unhcr.ch/refworld/pub/wpapers/wpno39.pdf (last checked by author February 2002)

United Nations (2000a) 'United Nations Convention Against Transnational Organized Crime', http://www.odccp.org/crime_cicp_convention.html# final (last checked by author February 2002)

United Nations (2000b) 'The Protocol to Prevent, Suppress and Punish Trafficking in Persons, Especially Women and Children, Supplementing the United Nations Convention Against Transnational Organized Crime' http://www.odccp.org/crime_cicp_convention.html#final (last checked by author February 2002)

United Nations (2000c) 'The Protocol to Prevent, Suppress and Punish Trafficking in Persons, Especially Women and Children, Supplementing the United Nations Convention Against Transnational Organized Crime', ratifications at: http://www.odccp.org/crime_cicp_signatures.html (last checked by author February 2002)

United Nations (2000d) 'The Protocol to Prevent, Suppress and Punish Trafficking in Persons, Especially Women and Children, Supplementing the United Nations Convention Against Transnational Organized Crime', with annotations: http://www.hrlawgroup.org/initiatives/trafficking_persons/ (last checked by author February 2002)

United Nations (2000e) 'Interpretative Notes for the Official Records (*Travaux Préparatoires*) of the Negotiation of the United Nations Convention Against Transnational Organized Crime and the Protocols', http://www.odccp.org/crime_cicp_convention_documents.html (last checked by author February 2002)

United Nations (2002) 'International Covenant on Economic, Social and Cultural Rights and International Covenant on Civil and Political Rights' http://www.unhcr.ch/html/intlinst.htm (last checked by the author February 2002)

Trafficking in children in West and Central Africa

Mike Dottridge

Trafficking of children between various African countries shot to prominence in April 2001 as a result of media reports that a ship carrying 'slave children', the Etireno, had gone missing after being refused permission to land at Libreville in Gabon. When the ship eventually docked in Cotonou in Benin, the port it had first sailed from, some journalists reported that no slaves were found on board. There were 43 trafficked children on the boat, not chained or visibly enslaved. They were accompanied by adults who initially claimed to be relatives, but who, after leaving the boat, did their best to disappear from view. Many of the children remained so intimidated that they did not dare recount the truth about where they came from to social workers at the shelters they were taken to, run by Terre des Hommes *and others. This article highlights media portrayal of trafficking in children in West and Central Africa, explains why girls are more likely to be trafficked, and discusses some counter-trafficking initiatives undertaken by a range of institutions.*

Poverty is a central factor in the decision of parents to send their children away to work. The prospect of good wages in a wealthier country, such as Gabon or Côte d'Ivoire, makes sending children away seem acceptable. The realities of what migrant or trafficked children have to face along the route and once they reach their destination are not widely known. However, poverty is not the only factor influencing the pattern of trafficking of children that occurs in West and Central Africa. The majority, particularly of younger trafficked children, are girls. There exists an assumption – common in other parts of the world as well – that girls are best suited for work in the house or linked to the household economy; that girls will leave their parental household on marriage; and that it is consequently not worth investing in their education or future to the same extent as it might be for boys.

Trafficking or slavery?

Many media reports in 2001 suggested that the trafficking of children between different West African countries was being revealed to the public for the first time, and one BBC journalist claimed that slavery was 'West Africa's dirty little secret'. The media attention also precipitated an expensive programme by the cocoa and chocolate industry to put its house in order. In practice, however, it was West African NGO activists and journalists who had done the bulk of the work in bringing the pattern of child trafficking in the region to light, as well as pioneering efforts to assist the children concerned.

Western media reports portrayed the problem as one of slavery, rather than 'mere' trafficking. The reality of today's slave trade in most parts of the world is that adults and children fleeing poverty or seeking better prospects are manipulated, deceived, and bullied into working in conditions that they would not choose. For this reason, the term 'trafficking' is usually more appropriate than 'slavery' – although some children and adults certainly do end up as slaves. The investigations in West Africa revealed that children, many of them younger than 12, were being moved between countries at an alarming rate. While some girls are trafficked into prostitution, most children go into other forms of work, with the majority of girls employed as domestic servants or street vendors. Some are paid, but many are not. In most cases, recruiters promise to send the children's parents some money, and in a few cases they hand over cash straight away. However, families do not 'sell' their children: they send them away in the hope that they will make their fortune in wealthier cities or countries overseas and – mistakenly – they trust the smooth-talking agents who paint a rosy picture of the children's prospects.

In numerous cases Western journalists reminded their audiences that the region where children were being enslaved was precisely the same 'Slave Coast' visited by ships involved historically in the Transatlantic slave trade. They seemed to be suggesting that West Africans are irredeemably attached to slavery as a way of recruiting cheap labour, although the sentiments were rarely voiced in such racist terms. Most reporters focused on the sectors where cruelty and exploitation were most visible – the horrendous experiences of children in transit and after arriving at their destinations. Very few visited the children's villages or towns of origin to report on the factors propelling children away.

Gender roles and inequality: a key factor

Cross-border trafficking of children got under way in West Africa on a significant scale in the 1980s, based on the region's traditions of migration and of 'placing' children to live and work with relatives and in better off households as part of their upbringing. In some cases, children sent to relatives helped with housework. By the late 1990s, however, it was clear that there was a regional market for child labour, with demand highest in relatively well-off areas such as Gabon, southwest Nigeria, and southern Côte d'Ivoire.

Demand for girls' labour in urban areas

The demand in urban areas appears to be significantly higher for girls than boys. Girls are sought by adult women, to work for them in the house, or to assist them in selling food and other products in the streets and markets. To some extent, therefore, in West Africa as elsewhere, the employment by women of other women or girls to carry out domestic chores is a sign of women's economic power.

Women employers not only say that girls are 'more obedient' than boys, and consequently preferred, but sometimes even know which ethnic group they prefer as the 'most obedient'. In contrast, the demand for boys seems to be lower in towns, as they are less frequently employed as domestic servants. However, boys are recruited to work on farms in Côte d'Ivoire and other areas, doing work that accords priority to physical strength. There is also an established pattern of trafficking of young Nigerian women from Edo State into prostitution in Europe, but that is not covered in this article.

Gender inequality and child placement

Undoubtedly, the West African tradition of 'placing' children in other people's households has been a major cultural factor encouraging trafficking (and in late 2001 this was said to be largely responsible for the large number of West African children living in Britain with families other than their own – reportedly around 10,000).[1] However, other traditions have aggravated the situation. The custom of girls marrying out, leaving their families and often their community when they get married, means that families are accustomed to daughters leaving the household and community at some point. Secondly, in communities where girls work in the home and are not kept in school to learn other skills, domestic service and early marriage become the only career paths available for many. Thirdly, rules of inheritance – particularly rules that exclude girls and women from owning or inheriting land – tend to marginalise girls and women in their communities of origin. An integrated strategy against trafficking should encompass these factors, as well as the poverty of many rural areas, the ease with which children can be moved across frontiers illegally, and the inclination of employers to exploit children who are not their own ruthlessly.

NGO research and investigations

As early as September 1996, Constitutional Rights Project, a Nigerian NGO, focused attention on child trafficking inside Nigeria, as well as into and out of the country, in a report entitled 'Modernised Slavery – Child Trade in Nigeria'. At about the same time, WAO-Afrique, an NGO based in Lomé (Togo) – which for several years had been assisting children brought from rural areas to work as domestic servants in Lomé – started investigating reports that large numbers of Togolese girls were being taken abroad to work as domestic servants, principally to Gabon (Effah 1996).

Reporting to a UN working group in May 1997 on their findings, WAO-Afrique's director, Cléophas Mally, recalled how his organisation's investigation of human trafficking was sparked by a letter from a young Togolese woman in Lebanon, complaining that she found herself in conditions amounting to slavery. While WAO-Afrique prepared to focus on the trafficking of young women to work as domestics in the Middle East, however, its investigators found that many more (and younger) Togolese girls were being exported to Gabon, an oil-exporting country in central Africa. Reporting to the UN, WAO-Afrique said it had found the following pattern:

> *'The traffic of children especially concerns young girls between the ages of eight and 12. Children as young as six have also been found. There is a very distinct preference on the part of parents to place girls rather than boys in the service of relatives, be they close or far away. According to the investigation, the phenomenon affects 80 per cent of children in rural environments, of which 75 per cent of the girls have never set foot in a school. More than 50 per cent of them are younger than 14 years old.'*[2]

The following year (April 1998) WAO-Afrique organised a seminar in Togo, to discuss its findings. This was the first occasion when officials from Benin and Togo met together to talk about the problem, together with representatives of NGOs and UNICEF. While Togolese government officials were at this point unwilling to even use the term 'trafficking' to describe the export of children, the Beninois authorities indicated that they were already active in trying to prevent children from being taken abroad, and had intercepted 700 children at border points during the first seven months of 1997 alone.

During 1998, others in West Africa took up the issue. An NGO in Benin, ESAM, (supported by Anti-Slavery International and Britain's National Lottery) investigated the situation of Beninois children taken to work in Gabon. Its investigators interviewed 138 trafficked children in Gabon, all but one of whom were girls. Other testimonies revealed that Beninois children were being held in transit at fishing villages in south-east Nigeria, before being embarked in open canoes to cross the sea to Libreville.

Also in 1998, a newspaper in Côte d'Ivoire denounced the trafficking of children from Burkina Faso and Mali into Côte d'Ivoire, and claimed that boys were being sold to work on farms for as little as US$30, producing a range of commercial crops (IVOIR'SOIR 1998, 18). The newspaper publicity led the governments of Côte d'Ivoire and Mali to set up a commission of inquiry and, in September 2000, to sign an agreement to curb the traffic.

UN and government responses

From 1998 onwards, inter-governmental organisations started taking an interest in the issue, starting with UNICEF, which held a sub-regional workshop on 'Trafficking in Child Domestic Workers, in particular Girls in Domestic Service in West and Central Africa', in July 1998. The ILO and the World Bank also became involved, as did the UN Centre for International Crime Prevention, working with ECOWAS (the Economic Community of West African States), to produce an ECOWAS Declaration and Plan of Action Against Trafficking in December 2001. Suddenly it seemed that the issue of child trafficking was one that every organisation had to be seen to be doing something about.

Within two years these international organisations were virtually tripping over each other to organise programmes and help local organisations – but there was (and is) little effective co-ordination between them. Each agrees that its general objective is to end trafficking of children, but their strategies for doing so differ and so make contradictory demands on the government and societies involved. Rather surprisingly, the agencies have given very little priority to identifying the best practical ways of protecting trafficked children once they are recognised, or to resolving the key question of whether to leave the children where they are, while improving their conditions, or whether to remove and repatriate them. One consequence is that a small and unofficial NGO based in Libreville is still tackling this challenge virtually on its own, without the resources or profile that support from international organisations could give it.

Conclusions

Virtually all of the research on trafficking of children in West and Central Africa suggests that the majority of trafficked children are girls. It is clear to investigators that gender issues are critical in determining which children are sent away by parents, and which are preferred for employment in urban households. Gender issues have been taken into account when programmes to prevent trafficking have been designed – programmes have stressed in particular the value of keeping girls in school as long as boys – but these are in their infancy.

However, West African policy makers' sensitivity and commitment to gender issues are much less obvious. At a very crude level, the region's governments assume that trafficking is an issue for whichever ministry deals with women's and girl's issues, rather than one which should be handled, for example, by the Ministry of Labour in the context of mainstream employment and child labour policies. The result so far has been that rather ineffective actions have been taken on a piecemeal basis in a way that would almost certainly be unacceptable if the majority of trafficking victims were men and boys.

Mike Dottridge is Director of Anti-Slavery International, Thomas Clarkson House, The Stableyard, Broomgrove Road, London SW9 9TL, United Kingdom. Tel: +44 (0)207 501 8920; fax +44 (0)207 738 4110;
E-mail: m.dottridge@antislavery.org
http://www.antislavery.org

Notes

1 This was reported on BBC Radio Four's *Today* programme in December 2001.

2 Cléophas Mally, Director of WAO Afrique, in a statement to the Working Group on Contemporary Forms of Slavery (22nd session, Geneva, June 1997) of the UN Sub-commission on Prevention of Discrimination and Protection of Minorities.

References

Effah, J. (1996) *Modernised Slavery – Child Trade in Nigeria,* Lagos: Constitutional Rights Project

Diaroukou, Sangho (1998) 'Trafic d'enfants maliens – les auteurs démasqués', *IVOIR'SOIR,* p.18, 18 May

Child marriage and child prostitution:
two forms of sexual exploitation

Susanne Louis B. Mikhail

This article highlights some of the similarities between child marriages and child prostitution. Both child marriage and prostitution involve economic transactions, lack of freedom, and the violation of a child's right to consent. This is often exacerbated by social and economic vulnerabilities of children linked to limited life options. In order to capture much of the ongoing discussion and debate taking place in North Africa and the Middle East, this article draws on anecdotal evidence, limited research samples, communication with local actors, and the author's own personal experiences in the region. It also discusses some initiatives undertaken by a range of institutions with the aim of preventing these practices.

The countries in North Africa and the Middle East differ markedly in their level of economic development, political climate, degree of secularism, and social structures. However, there are some areas of social life where general attitudes and beliefs are similar in many countries. Child marriages and child prostitution are two such areas.

Traditionally, child marriages and child prostitution have been regarded as being in moral opposition to each other. While early marriages have been respected and valued as desirable and honorable, prostitution has been denounced as an absolute disgrace, and in religious circles has usually been condemned as a sin. The honour attached to early marriage has traditionally been linked to its most central purpose: the assurance of virginity at the time of marriage.[1] In addition, early marriage is a way of preventing girls from initiating intimate relations with unfamiliar men. Conversely, child prostitution endorses intimate contact with often unfamiliar men.

Shifting attitudes to early marriage

However, time has dramatically modified these general attitudes such that early marriages in general and child marriage in particular are increasingly frowned upon in many Middle Eastern and North African countries. This change has been manifested in various international statements. The African Charter on the Rights and of the Welfare of the Child, drafted in 1990, states that, 'Child marriage and the betrothal of girls and boys shall be prohibited, and effective action including legislation shall be taken to specify the minimum age of marriage to be 18 years.' The Inter-African Committee on Traditional Practices Affecting the Health of Women and Children states that early marriage is 'any marriage carried out below the age of 18, before the girl is physically, physiologically and psychologically ready to shoulder the responsibilities of marriage and child bearing'.

Not only is child marriage becoming a source of criticism: the discourse of comparing child marriages with child prostitution is also taking a new course.

Increasingly, it is argued that the differences between child marriage and child prostitution are neither as many nor as profound as they were traditionally regarded to be, and that both practices share a number of characteristics. This approach, once promoted by a few, avant-garde NGOs and human rights advocates, is now spreading within the general public, political establishment, and cultural elites.

In October 2001, the government of Morocco held the 'Pan-African Forum Against the Sexual Exploitation of Children' in Rabat. Delegates from 65 countries were amenable to the idea of identifying child marriages in general and forced child marriages in particular as a type of commercial sexual exploitation of children (child prostitution included). Although this approach was primarily espoused by NGOs and human rights lawyers, government representatives were increasingly in agreement with this outlook.

This article outlines ongoing discussions concerning child marriage and child prostitution taking place in North Africa and the Middle East. Due to the sensitivity surrounding the issues, it has been difficult to conduct substantial research, and research studies and estimates are often based on anecdotal evidence and limited samples. As a result, I have chosen to refer only sparingly to statistical data, as they are often inadequate and not absolutely reliable. Instead, I have relied on personal field experiences, and communications with various local actors. As a result of the widespread silence of national legislation on these issues, and their prevalence in social and religious debate, I have chosen to use religious texts and documentation as sources of reference.

Economic transactions: beneficiaries and losers

Prostitution is characterised by an economic transaction, usually between the supplier and their client. Similarly, child marriages often involve an economic transaction between the client and supplier. This traditional practice is however explicitly prohibited by the 1956 Supplementary Convention on the Abolition of Slavery, the Slave Trade, and Institutions and Practices Similar to Slavery. Article 1 states the institutions and practices similar to slavery where, 'a woman, without the right to refuse, is promised or given in marriage on payment of a consideration in money or in kind to her parents [or] guardian family...'.

Dowry payments

In North Africa and the Middle East, the institution of dowry complicates the situation. The Koraan states that the husband must pay a '*mahr*' to his future wife. The *mahr* is prevalent in all Muslim marriages, but in marriages between two adults (where there is a higher degree of equality between the partners), it has less significance and is usually channeled through practical arrangements: for example, husbands might buy the flat while wives contribute to interior furnishing and contents. Thus, there is a sense of balance and the *mahr* is reciprocated by the bride's contribution. Mutual contributions to practical items are also common among the Christians in North Africa and the Middle East. In poor areas, however, where child marriage is most prevalent, the dowry becomes of great importance. It turns into a one-way transaction, a clear-cut payment.

With both child marriages and child prostitution, exchanged payments are most frequently received by a third party, and not the girl herself. In child prostitution, the 'owner/employer' of the child usually receives the payment. Normally he or she passes on only a small amount to the girl. In child marriages, a girl usually receives nothing at all. The third party, usually her parents, receives the whole amount. Ironically, the dowry received on the marriage of a daughter is quite often used to pay for the dowry of a son's future bride.

Though national laws do not regulate this kind of payment, the Koraan itself is quite explicit about dowry. Verse 4:004 states, 'And give the *women* [on their marriage] their dower as a free gift, but if they, of their good pleasure, remit any part of it to you, take it and enjoy it with right good cheer.' Clearly, the dowry should be paid to the woman, in this case the child.

Siqueh *and short-term contract marriages*

The economic transaction in child marriages is more similar to that of child prostitution in the case of short term/short contract marriages. For example, in Iran, a man can marry a female for a short period of time, ranging from hours to months. This system called *siqueh*, was originally put in place to assist war widows who had had no other means of supporting their families. But as the legal age for marriage is 13.8, this practice has actually become a way for men to initiate pseudo-legalised child marriages, that may last for only a few hours.

In Egypt there is a similar phenomenon, which has traditionally been ignored because of its sensitivity. However, last year the Ministry of Social Affairs, in joint efforts with UNICEF, investigated this specific type of child marriage. The study focused on a village near Cairo, which is well known for marrying its young girls to much older men from Arab countries. Usually the men marry these girls for a short period – typically during the summer months – at the end of which the men go back to their countries, where it is very hard to trace them. The girls remain in their villages, and in many cases they give birth to children. The legal age of consent to marriage, which is 16, may be circumvented in a number of ways, including falsifying the girl's age with a doctor's certificate, using the birth certificate of a deceased older sister, or registering the marriage only after the bride has turned 16. A further problem is that in the last decade the phenomenon has taken on a highly commercial form, as broker markets have emerged for young girls to be contracted into 'marriage' to wealthy men from the Arab Gulf countries. The agents operate undercover, introducing the families of prospective brides to their future husbands, whereupon a contract is drawn between the two parties. Since the marriage is illegal it is not registered, the main point of negotiation being the amount of the *mahr* (dowry). These women's social and economic status does not improve after marriage. They often find out that their principal role is to serve the other wives of the wealthy man, or they are left to fend for themselves and any resulting children after their husband disappears when the summer vacation is over (Tilgay and Sarhan 2001).

The Ministry of Social Affairs conducted a study in the summer of 2001 with 35 women in Badrashen and Hawamdeya, two districts in the municipality of Giza. In these two districts, broker markets are well established. The figures – which are not representative for Egypt as a whole, because of the remoteness of these districts – show that of the 35 women interviewed, 46 per cent had married before they were 16, 29 per cent of whom married a husband aged over 55.

Abduction and temporary marriage

In countries where there are conflicts, child marriages sometimes take the form of a combination of child prostitution and pure slavery. In Algeria, Sudan, and Chad, young women have been abducted by militias or gangsters and are subjected to sexual abuse and violence in what the kidnappers call 'temporary marriages'. In fact, this is a form of slavery in which the girls have no rights whatsoever. However, these acts are also condemned by the Koraan which states in verse 24: 033: '... and if any of you slaves ask for a deed in writing [to enable them to earn their freedom for a certain sum] give them such a deed if ye know any good in them... but force not your maids to prostitution when they desire chastity...'.

Lack of consent: powerlessness and violation of rights

Very few girls are informed of where they are heading, when they are brought into prostitution. Those that have some kind of idea of the impact it will have on their lives are usually very reluctant. Girls are not given the opportunity to give their consent or otherwise in a decision that will affect their entire life. Similarly, in child marriages, girls are usually not given a chance to give their consent. This is instead given by their parents.

Few parents seek intentionally to harm their children; usually the lack of the child's consent is justified by reference to a general belief that parents know best in these matters. But this kind of argument can only work where adult daughters have excellent communication and friendly relationships with their parents. In this situation, parents as well as friends and others can offer substantial advice. However, in child marriages, which most often occur in poor areas where parents are responsible for a great number of children, the child bride-to-be may be just one of many children and not a priority. More importantly, at the age of 12 or 14 – when most girls are neither physically nor psychologically mature for childbearing – no man whomsoever is suitable.

Denying children the right to consent to marriage is a violation of their rights and a crime according to several international declarations. Article 16 of the 1948 Universal Declaration on Human Rights states that 'Marriage shall be entered into only with free and full consent of the intending parties.' Article 1 of the 1964 Convention on Consent to Marriage, Minimum age of Marriage and Registration of Marriage, states that, 'No marriage shall be legally entered into without the full and free consent of both parties, such consent to be expressed by them in person as prescribed by law.' Moreover, article 16.1 of the 1979 Convention on the Elimination of All Forms of Discrimination against Women prescribes for both men and women an equal right to enter marriage, choose a spouse, and enter marriage only with their free and full consent. Finally, the Convention of the Rights of the Child – which has been ratified by all Middle Eastern and North African countries – stresses 'the right of children to have their views taken into account in matters that concern them'.

The national legislation of the countries in the Middle East and North Africa is generally lacking in terms of the protection of the right to consent to marriage. However, since religious authorities are often more highly regarded and respected than legal instruments, they are in a position to use their power of influence with reference to verse 4:019 in the Koraan. 'O ye who believe! Ye are forbidden to inherit women against their will.'

Involving a girl in a marriage without her consent can have dramatic effects on her entire life and all her future prospects to become an equal decision maker in the home. The lack of her consent gives a signal to her husband and to society as a whole that her opinion is unimportant.

Lives of bondage

Child prostitutes worldwide are often bonded to their owner or employer. Children's vulnerability means that their freedom to choose whether to stay or leave is extremely restricted. In most cases, the child is seen as a possession or object that has been bought and is therefore not entitled to liberty. This kind of bondage is further intensified in contexts where extreme social stigma is associated with prostitution. In other regions such as Asia or Latin America, some children are engaged in prostitution yet still maintain a relationship with their family, often because of the child's role as a family supporter and financial contributor. In the Middle East, however, this is exceptionally rare. A child engaged in prostitution is deprived of all ties to their community, rejected by their family, and is left with few or no options other than to stay in prostitution.

Similarly, when a girl has been given away as a bride, she is considered to be her husband's possession and bonded for life. This is particularly the case in societies where considerable stigma attaches to divorce. Some North African and Middle Eastern countries, such as Egypt and Tunisia, give girls the right to divorce, but in reality this is difficult. More often, they are trapped, experiencing early and frequent childbirth, and vulnerable to domestic violence.

In Egypt, 29 per cent of married adolescents have been beaten by their husbands and, of these, 41 per cent have been beaten during pregnancy. In Jordan, 26 per cent of reported cases of domestic violence were committed against wives under 18. The dangerous effects of early pregnancy and childbirth are widely accepted to include increased risk of dying, and increased risk of premature labour and severe complications during delivery. Pregnancy-related deaths are the leading cause of mortality for 15-19-year-old girls (married or unmarried) worldwide. Those under age 15 are five times more likely to die than women in their twenties (UNICEF 2001). According to the Egyptian Ministry of Social Affairs, the mortality rate of adolescent mothers is 60 per cent higher than that of mothers over 24 (Tilgay and Sarhan 2001).

The general public has little consideration for (or is simply unaware of) international declarations that support women's right to divorce. Article 16 of the 1948 Universal Declaration on Human Rights states that, 'Men and women of full age have the right to found a family. They are entitled to equal rights as to consent to marriage, during marriage and its dissolution.' In most Islamic societies, men are entitled to ask for divorce, while women do not have similar legal rights. In those countries where legal mechanisms are being developed, for example, Egypt (which is granting similar legal rights to women), practical implementation is very difficult for social and economic reasons. A girl may find herself trapped within a marriage because she sees no other means of survival.

Loss of adolescence, forced sexual relations, and the denial of freedom and personal development have profound psychological and emotional consequences (UNICEF 2001). Nevertheless, most girls in such situations have nowhere to go as they are surrounded by people who endorse their situation.

Economic and social vulnerability

Children engaged in prostitution, and those who are married, encounter tremendous difficulties in changing their situation. Some few girls show exceptional strength (or exceptional desperation), either persuading their husbands to divorce them, or simply running away. However, those few who manage to escape – whether prostitutes or married / divorced – often find that their future is characterised by extreme economic and social vulnerability.

Economic vulnerability

Economic vulnerability exists because of the lack of alternative work and livelihood opportunities for girls who are usually under-educated and under-skilled. Child prostitutes and married children have often been deprived of substantial education opportunities. A girl who marries becomes a housewife with limited opportunities to continue her education. While child prostitutes have a theoretical possibility of attending school, as their 'working hours' are usually during the night, in practice this is difficult for various reasons. First, the 'owner' usually refuses to expose the child to the public for fear of people noticing the kind of activity that the child is engaged in.

This is particularly the case in Middle Eastern and North African countries where the penalties connected with prostitution are extremely severe – in some cases the death penalty – and prostitution occurs undercover as a result. In addition, child prostitutes are often involved in household work during the day, or lack the energy and capacity required for schoolwork.

Child marriage and child prostitution deny children of school age their right to the education. This in turn hinders their potential to earn an income. Consequently, child marriages and prostitution contribute to the 'feminisation of poverty' (UNICEF 2001).

Child marriage is also linked to a high degree of wife abandonment, which leaves girls in a vulnerable situation. This case is particularly relevant for short term/short contract marriages. The study that was conducted by the Egyptian Ministry of Social Affairs revealed that of the 35 women interviewed, 67 per cent had subsequently divorced. None of these women received any of the financial assistance to which they were entitled by the Koraan. Verse 002:241 assures that 'For divorced women maintenance [should be provided] on a reasonable [scale].'

Social vulnerability

Child prostitutes and married children may both be exposed to community exclusion and/or physical threats. Girls who insist on divorce usually experience isolation or abandonment. In many cases they are punished through family-related violence, and in extreme cases their lives are threatened. They run the risk of the so-called 'honour killing'. Lately, however, there have been some serious efforts by governments to outlaw such practices. Egypt and Jordan have been frontrunners in combating 'honour killing' through tougher legal measures.

Child prostitutes, on the other hand, often break free from prostitution only to find themselves placed in institutions or prisons. As these girls are seen as public goods, they become subjected to physical violence and sexual abuse in the very institutions that are supposed to protect them and help them in the recovery process.

Conclusions

In comparison with other regions such as South-East Asia, Eastern Europe, or Sub-Saharan Africa, child prostitution is still very limited in North Africa and the Middle East. Not surprisingly, poverty is the major contributory factor to children's vulnerability to sexual exploitation. Children of the middle and upper classes, and educated children in big cities such as Cairo, Amman, and Beirut have more protection and can be better informed of their rights. Children in war-torn countries are more at risk of sexual exploitation, as they live in societies where some degree of anarchy and breakdown of social protection and controls prevails. There are links between conflicts in Algeria and Sudan and the increase in sexual vulnerability of children.

Cultural and social taboos in many Middle Eastern and North African countries have hindered the practical administration of sound and adequate research. Child prostitution is practised to a much lesser extent than child marriage. Most countries have realised the paramount importance of protecting children from commercial sexual exploitation, and some very harsh penalty measures have been introduced to combat child prostitution. Despite the rising awareness of the harm associated with child marriages, very little has been practically implemented to combat this form of exploitation.

The above-mentioned legal situation creates an extraordinary and contradictory climate where a man who sexually abuses a child can on the one hand be sentenced to death (if it is a matter of child rape or child prostitution), but on the other backed up by legal instruments and social approval (if he chooses to marry the child).

However, as demonstrated in Rabat in October 2001, most governments are currently in the process of reviewing their national legislation to offer stronger and more comprehensive support for children. In addition, NGOs and human rights groups are progressively and courageously committed to upholding the rights of the child, while religious authorities become increasingly critical of child marriages.[2]

It is important to bear in mind that boys are also subjected to child prostitution and child marriages, and that they too need the same kinds of protection. However, as this article has demonstrated the social construction of women's and girls' roles, responsibilities, and relations mean that they typically have less control over their lifes, and fewer life choices and options.

Susanne Louis B. Mikhail is Regional Officer for North Africa, the Middle East, and Central Asia at ECPAT International, 328 Phya Thai Road, Ratchatevi, Bangkok 10400, Thailand. E-mail: susannem@ecpat.net

Notes

1 The significance of virginity is further manifested by other practices such as female genital mutilation (FGM) – which has been prohibited in a number of Middle Eastern and North African countries, such as Egypt and Mauritania – and 'virginity reconstruction', a practice intended to reconstruct female sex organs to give the impression that a girl is a virgin, though she has had sexual intercourse. Both operations pose considerable risks to girls' health.

2 I feel obliged to mention that though all cases of child prostitution I have encountered have been destructive, some child marriages have appeared to be happy. In these cases the parents have been genuinely interested in the well-being of their child, the husbands have been caring and supportive, and the children have been given a chance to give their consent, and had the opportunity to complete their education. But these cases are rare. In the best circumstances the girl is indifferent, and mostly she is discouraged and wants to escape, but is unable to do so. I have listened to several first-hand stories and many child complaints, and they all express similar fears and distress.

References

Tilgay, C. and D. Sarhan (2001) 'Early marriages amongst girls in Egypt; a hidden phenomenom?', *Insight Magazine*, March, p.49

UNICEF (2001) 'Early Marriage, Child Spouses', *Innocenti Digest* 7: March

Slavery and gender:
women's double exploitation

Beth Herzfeld

For many people, the word slavery conjures up images from history – of the transatlantic slave trade, the practice of buying and selling people that the modern world is supposed to have left behind, and of the 19th century abolitionist movement. But the reality is that not only does slavery exist today, it is expanding. An estimated 27 million women, children, and men are currently enslaved around the world (Bales 1999, 8): Eastern European women are bonded into prostitution in Western Europe; children are trafficked between West African countries; and men are forced to work as slaves on Brazilian agricultural estates. Contemporary slavery can affect people of any age, sex, or race on every continent and in most countries. This article is an introduction to what constitutes slavery. It focuses on bonded labour (the most widespread form of slavery today), and on the worst forms of child labour. It provides examples of the way in which socially constructed expectations can increase women's and children's vulnerability to slavery-like practices.

What is slavery?

Contemporary slavery takes many forms: bonded labour, forced labour, forced and early marriage, the worst forms of child labour, human trafficking, and 'traditional' slavery. All types of slavery share some of the following key elements, with persons being:

- forced to work through the threat or use of violence;
- owned or controlled by an 'employer', usually through mental, physical, or threatened abuse;
- dehumanised, treated as a commodity, or even bought and sold as 'property';
- physically constrained or having restrictions placed on their freedom of movement and freedom to change employment.

A person can be subject to more than one form of slavery at a given time. In some cases, a person is enslaved for several months, in others they may be enslaved for their whole lives, passing the status on to their children. For example, in the case of bonded labour (also known as debt bondage) a debt that keeps individuals or families enslaved can be passed on from generation to generation.

Gender-specific forms of slavery

Poverty, greed, marginalisation – particularly of women and girls and of minority groups – social complicity, and lack of political will to address the issue, are central to slavery's existence. Although slavery affects men, women, and children, there are particular slavery-like practices that are gender-specific.

Female ritual servitude, which is found in West Africa, is one example of this. Under the system of *Trokosi* in south-eastern Ghana, girls as young as seven are given by their family to a shrine in order to atone for a family transgression. The family believes that if they do not do this, they will be cursed; this 'contract' can last for generations.

As one former *Trokosi* recounted:

'I was sent to the shrine when I was nine years old because my grandmother stole a pair of earrings. I was made to work from dawn until dusk in the fields and when I came home there was no food for me to eat. When I was 11, the priest made his first attempt to sleep with me. I refused and was beaten mercilessly. The other girls in the shrine told me it was going to keep happening and if I refused I would be beaten to death and the next time he tried I gave in. The suffering was too much so I tried to escape to my parents but they wouldn't accept me and sent me back to the shrine. I couldn't understand how my parents could be so wicked.'
(Anti-Slavery International 2000, 11)

Although the girls themselves have not committed any crime, they are obliged to work all day in the priest's fields and are forced to act as a wife to him, including providing sexual services. The priest keeps several *Trokosi* at a time. In effect, the priest exercises ownership over them.

More generally, social and cultural factors play a role in gender decisions over whether girls or boys are sent out to work in order to send money back to the family. Because it is expected that girls in many societies will leave the home at a future date by marrying into another family, girls are often less valued and seen as more dispensable than boys. In some cultures, dowry payments are considered a financial drain, meaning that a daughter is seen as a burden to (and by) her family. Sending young girls away to work is a way of lightening the burden of a poor household. The work they go to do is seen as suited to girls and women; often it is house-based work (domestic labour), involves making and selling food, or is sex work. In all forms of slavery, women and girls are subject to particular abuse and treatment because of their gender. In the next section, bonded labour, and the additional hardships faced by women who are bonded, are examined.

Bonded labour and gender issues

According to the United Nations Working Group on Contemporary Forms of Slavery, at least 20 million people around the world are affected by bonded labour (United Nations 1999, 36). Bonded labour is most prevalent in South Asia, but it is also found in other regions including the Americas and Europe.

People become bonded when their labour is demanded as a means of repayment for a loan, or for money given in advance. Usually they are forced by necessity or are tricked into taking a loan in order to pay for such basic needs as food, medicine, and for social obligations such as the costs of a wedding or funeral. Some take loans in order to finance their migration, in search of a higher income elsewhere. To repay the loan, bonded labourers are typically forced to work long hours regardless of their age or health, sometimes for seven days a week, 365 days a year.

In South Asia, entire families can be bonded, requiring children, as well as adults, to work. And once the loan is taken, bonded labourers are deprived of their rights to negotiate terms and conditions of work. They are charged high rates of interest, and because they do not even receive a minimum wage, the cycle of interest and debt keeps them enslaved. Most have no proof of their agreement and, if a contract exists, few can read it, leaving them vulnerable to continued exploitation.

The practice has its roots in South Asia's caste system, and a disproportionate number are *dalits* (those at the bottom of the caste hierarchy) and members of tribal groups. In industries such as agriculture and quarrying, in some South Asian countries, the vast majority of those working as bonded labourers come from those groups.

Women's additional hardship

Although all bonded labourers are vulnerable to abuse, women suffer additional hardship due to their low social status. They not only have to work long hours in the fields and undertake domestic chores in their husband's employer's home, but they must also fulfil domestic duties in their own home.

When a husband becomes a bonded labourer, it is not unusual for his wife's labour to be automatically included with the man's as repayment by an employer. And among bonded labourers, women and girls are particularly vulnerable to rape by landlords.

Pultalingamma, aged 45 (interviewed in 1999), has worked as a bonded labourer in India for more than 25 years.

> *'My husband died five years ago as a bonded labourer. Now I bear the responsibility of repaying both of our loans ..... I go to work at 6am, cleaning the cattle shed and performing domestic chores in the landlord's house. Then I go to work in the fields, and return at the end of the day to resume domestic chores. I return home between six and eight pm to cook for my own children ..... I will make sure my daughter stays in school. I won't let her go and work for the landlord because he will "spoil" her.'*
>
> (Anti-Slavery International 1999)

The feudal aspect of bonded labour means that the person who owes the debt is effectively owned while the debt is held. While a man may nominally take a loan himself, his wife and children may in fact be included in the contract. The slave-owner sees the slave as there to satisfy all of his needs – labour and otherwise, meaning that women are particularly vulnerable to abuse

In addition to women, children are also vulnerable, as they are seen as easy to control. They are subject to exploitation that can harm their health and welfare. Work in this category constitutes the worst forms of child labour.

The worst forms of child labour

The International Labour Organization estimates that of the 250 million (ILO 1996) children aged between five and 14 who work in developing countries, 120 million (*op. cit.*) work full-time, and 80 million (ILO 1999, 2) are in work that is harmful to their mental and physical well-being. These figures do not include the number of children who are engaged in the worst forms of child labour in Europe and North America.

According to the International Labour Organization's Convention No. 182, on the Worst Forms of Child Labour (1999), a child includes anyone under the age of 18, with no exceptions (Article 2) (Brown 2001, 5). The definition of the worst forms of child labour includes:

- all forms of slavery or similar practices, such as debt bondage, trafficking, and forced or compulsory recruitment of children for use in armed conflict;
- the use of children for prostitution and pornography;
- the use of children for illicit activities, such as the production and trafficking of drugs;
- all work which is likely to endanger the health, safety, or morality of children (Article 3) (*ibid*).

Although some types of work can contribute positively to a child's development as well as providing a vital source of income helping to sustain the child and their family, millions of children around the world are forced into work that is damaging or extremely exploitative. They are denied their right to education, and their physical and mental health – and even their lives – are put at risk.

Gender differences in child labour practices

Exploitative employers often prefer children to adults because they are more vulnerable, easier to control, cheaper, and less likely to demand better working conditions and higher wages. Most working children around the world work in agriculture, although the single largest form of employment for girls worldwide is domestic work in the homes of strangers. This reflects the general cultural view that girls are well-suited for employment in domestic work. They also sell food in open markets, and are 'sold off' into sex work. Boys are more likely to be involved in farming and animal herding, quarries (though girls in Nepal also work as stone-breakers), fishing, and some factory work. In South Asia, however, girls make bangles, and both boys and girls make carpets in small 'factories'.

In some cases the children or their parents are tricked by traffickers' false promises of good, well-paid work and training, in others they are abducted, as is the case with some child camel jockeys and the children forced to fight for Uganda's main insurgent group, the Lord's Resistance Army (LRA). Boys as young as four from Pakistan, Bangladesh, and parts of Africa are abducted and taken to the Middle East to be camel jockeys. Desired because they are small and light, they are not paid. Before a race, they are deprived of food to keep them as light as possible. There are examples of abuse, severe injuries, and death.

In northern Uganda, abducted children – boys and girls – are believed to constitute 90 per cent of the LRA (Coalition Against the Use of Child Soldiers 1999, 114). Boys are used for fighting, looting villages, and abducting other children. Girls, who are also trained as soldiers, are mainly distributed to LRA soldiers as sex slaves (or 'wives') (*op. cit.*, 115). If they refuse, they are killed.

Children who work away from their families are particularly vulnerable because they are under the complete control of their employer. They work long hours for little or no pay and in many cases they sleep where they work. Roushan [not her real name], now 14, was trafficked from Bangladesh to India when she was ten years old. She was taken to the border and sold to a woman for 500 *taka* (US$6) who then sold her to a bangle factory.

> *'I didn't know how to make the bangles very well, which caused me to be beaten up. There were also older girls there who were threatened that if they didn't work well, they would bring men who would abuse them....'*

Between 100–150 girls and young women were locked in the house where they worked. They worked long hours and slept there. No beds or pillows were provided, so Roushan slept sitting against the wall, she said (Anti-Slavery 2001).

Working towards ending slavery

Despite the scale of slavery, change is possible. Anti-Slavery International, the world's oldest international human rights organisation, works at the local, national, and international levels to eliminate forms of slavery around the world.

At the international and national levels, Anti-Slavery presses governments that are not enforcing existing legislation to implement it. International and domestic laws prohibiting slavery do exist. Key international standards include the 1948 Universal Declaration of Human Rights, which applies to all United Nations member states. It prohibits the practice of slavery in all of its forms. The UN Supplementary Convention on the Abolition of Slavery, the Slave Trade, and Institutions and Practices Similar to Slavery (1956), which most states have ratified, and the International Labour Convention No. 29 concerning Forced or Compulsory Labour (1930), form the key international instruments banning bonded labour. But the lack of political will to enforce these laws and develop or implement domestic legislation allows such slavery as bonded labour to continue.

Children are further protected under Article 32 of the UN Convention on the Rights of the Child (1989) which states: 'States Parties recognize the right of the child to be protected from economic exploitation and from performing any work that is likely to be hazardous or to interfere with the child's education or to be harmful to the child's health or physical, mental, spiritual, moral, or social development.' In 1999, the International Labour Organization's Convention No. 82 on the Worst Forms of Child Labour defined which of 'the worst forms of child labour' it is an absolute priority to eradicate. Anti-Slavery International works with local partner organisations around the world to encourage governments to ratify and implement this measure.

In cases where legislation does not exist, we urge governments to develop workable laws and advocate for their enforcement. In many cases, slavery such as bonded labour and the practice of using children as domestics or to sell items in the market is so established it is not perceived to be a problem. Raising awareness in the countries concerned is crucial if the public is to support initiatives to end this abuse. There are a number of examples where raised awareness has led to significant changes. Anti-Slavery's partner in Togo, WAO Afrique, for example, has enabled communities to realise the dangers of child domestic labour by educating employers and children about children's rights. It also provides former child domestics with training to give them alternatives and to help them to avoid abusive employment.

Conclusion

If the elimination of slavery is to be effective, viable alternatives need to be made available for freed slaves, and the issue of poverty needs to be addressed. In Nepal, where in 2000 the government declared bonded labour illegal, thousands of freed bonded labourers were forced off the land. They have had to live in makeshift camps, on roadsides, and in forests because the government has both failed to provide assistance and to allocate land despite its promises. As a result their freedom has little meaning.

Slaves need to be empowered to free themselves. This is particularly relevant in the case of women and girls who are enslaved and who live in societies where women have low social status. In such situations it can be effective to challenge society's views of women and girls, as well as providing training programmes and poverty alleviation schemes to empower women and develop their confidence in themselves.

The forces of poverty, marginalisation, and social complicity which lead to exploitation need to be addressed if slavery is to be eliminated. Solutions must take into account the super-exploitation of women, particularly where families are enslaved, and also the underlying low status of women in many countries, which helps provide the conditions in which slavery can flourish.

Beth Herzfeld is Press Officer at Anti-Slavery International, Thomas Clarkson House, The Stableyard, Broomgrove Road, London, SW9 9TL, United Kingdom.
E-mail: antislavery@antislavery.org; http://www.antislavery.org

References

Anti-Slavery International (1999) *Interview with Pultalingamma*, April, India: Anti-Slavery International

Anti-Slavery International (2000) *Reporter*, Series VIII, 6: 1, January

Anti-Slavery International (2001) *Interview with Roushan*, November, London: Anti-Slavery International

Bales, Kevin (1999) *Disposable People: New Slavery in the Global Economy*, Berkeley: University of California Press

Brown, Pins (2001) *The New ILO Worst Forms of Child Labour Convention 1999: Do You Know...?*, Geneva NGO Group for the Convention on the Rights of the Child Sub-Group on Child Labour, Geneva: Anti-Slavery International

Coalition Against the Use of Child Soldiers (1999) *The Use of Child Soldiers in Africa: A Country Analysis of Child Recruitment and Participation in Armed Conflict*, London: Coalition Against the Use of Child Soldiers

International Labour Organization (ILO) (1996) Press Release, 12 November 1996, Geneva: ILO

International Labour Organization (ILO) (1999) *A New Tool to Combat the Worst Forms of Child Labour: ILO Convention 182*, Geneva: International Labour Office

United Nations (1999) *Report of the Working Group on Contemporary Forms of Slavery*, 24th Session, 1999, E/CN.4/Sub. 2/1999/17, 20th July, Geneva: United Nations Economic and Social Council

Half-hearted protection:
what does victim protection really mean for victims of trafficking in Europe?

Elaine Pearson

Anna (not her real name) was trafficked into forced prostitution from Eastern into Western Europe. She was 'rescued' during a police raid for being in the country illegally, and at the moment of arrest was given two choices: either make a statement against the trafficker and gain a temporary right of residence to stay in that country in order to testify; or else return back to her home country immediately. In this paper I look at the kind of measures taken in some European Union countries to protect trafficked persons,[1] particularly regarding temporary rights to stay for victims of trafficking, and suggest what else needs to be taken into account in order to combat the problem more effectively.

Imagine if victims of rape or torture could only get medical attention if they agreed to co-operate with the police in prosecuting their abusers? Why then is Anna's ultimatum still the standard approach by law enforcement officials to situations of trafficking throughout the world today? With the introduction of a new United Nations Protocol to Prevent, Suppress and Punish Trafficking in Persons, Especially Women and Children[2] in December 2000, trafficking in people, especially women and children is an issue increasingly on the national agenda of governments everywhere. Much of this attention has focused on creating new laws or ensuring that current laws are used to prosecute traffickers for their crimes. Protecting the interests of those who are trafficked has been a secondary priority, and for the most part has been prioritised only insofar as victims are aiding prosecutions. In Europe, for example, several countries have laws allowing trafficking victim-witnesses to be given the right to stay in the country of destination for the purpose of giving testimony and to receive various support services during that time. For those who do not testify however, options are generally limited to returning home.

Particularly for women, the 'option' of returning home presents a myriad of problems. The sexual violence suffered by many trafficked women increases their need for immediate protection and support such as medical care, counselling, and legal advice. Another consideration is the effect of moral attitudes towards sex, in their countries of origin. In Anna's case, for example, her family was unaware that she had been trafficked into prostitution. She knew that if they found out that she had been forced to work as a prostitute she would be shunned by her family and her entire community at home. Thus, it is important to bear in mind the specific issues raised for women, who are a majority of those trafficked.

Victim protection models: a right to stay

In several European countries, such as Belgium and the Netherlands,[3] the focus on protection of victims has been concerned with ensuring the temporary right to stay for victims. This stemmed from an early acknowledgement that a major barrier to successfully securing the conviction of traffickers was the inability or unwillingness of victims to testify. Victims were being deported or removed without any opportunity to report their trafficker, much less testify in court against them. Their unwillingness was due, amongst many things, to the fear of reprisals by the traffickers against themselves and their family, and also because victims of trafficking are often already severely traumatised.

Both Belgium and the Netherlands introduced changes to their immigration laws to grant all victims a 'breathing space', a period of time during which they could recover from their ordeal before making a more informed decision about whether or not to testify against the trafficker. The recovery period is 45 days in Belgium, and three months in the Netherlands. In both countries, extended temporary residence status was offered for those victims who agree to testify. During the period of stay, various support services are made available to trafficked persons, such as housing, medical and legal services, counselling, language and integration courses, financial assistance, and in Belgium, the right to work. Such measures were instituted because it was understood that if victims were given some time for reflection, and provided with appropriate care and support, they would be more likely to report their traffickers. The experience of both countries has shown this to be true, as more victims have reported their traffickers under the revised laws.

The European Union is now considering adopting a Directive regarding short term permits for victims of trafficking based on the Belgian model. Again, the objective is to encourage victims to testify against their traffickers.[4]

Limitations

While Belgium and the Netherlands have certainly led the way by initiating such protection mechanisms, some time has passed since the introduction of these measures in each country. The Dutch law was amended in 1988 and the Belgian law in 1995. We can now see the clear limitations of these measures, and these need to be addressed in any new proposed measures to protect trafficked persons, many of whom are women.

Firstly, the Belgian and Dutch models draw a distinction between those who testify and those who do not, with the end result that those who testify are 'rewarded' (by temporary residence and thus access to support services in the country), and those who do not are 'penalised' (by being forced to return home and potentially exposed to threats or reprisals by the traffickers, or simply returned into the same conditions from which they were originally trafficked). Undoubtedly, the need for protection increases as victims make the decision to testify against their traffickers, but that does not mean that those who do *not* testify (out of fear, or because they are too traumatised or lack sufficient information) should simply be repatriated.

Secondly, the Dutch and Belgian models are for the most part temporary, tied to the duration of the criminal proceedings. Under Dutch law, there is a right to permanent residence on 'humanitarian grounds', but this has been so narrowly construed that it is very rarely ever used successfully to attain permanent residence for trafficked persons. In Belgium, it is possible for a victim to stay longer if the prosecution is successful or if s/he proves that s/he has become integrated into Belgian society. The need for protection certainly does not end when the trial ends. In a successful case, traffickers may be sentenced and imprisoned, but the nature of trafficking as organised crime means that victims or their families are still likely to be threatened or attacked by other members of the network. For protection to be effective, whether in country of origin or destination, it needs to be longer lasting than the duration of a court case, and it needs to extend beyond the victim to include those close to her.

Governments must address the harm to which trafficked persons are subjected when they return home, regardless of whether they testify. This harm may range from actions of the state to actions of the individual (the trafficker). It has been reported that trafficked women returning to Nigeria from Italy, for example, have been held in detention facilities, forced to undergo medical examinations including tests for HIV/AIDS, and had their faces and names exposed in the media. The end result is that families and often entire communities ostracise returned trafficked women. In the Ukraine, Anti-Slavery International has heard at least one report of corrupt police, given the task of 'protecting' trafficked women, extorting money from returned women by threatening to tell their families that they were engaged in prostitution. There is the additional threat posed by the trafficker or those in their network who may threaten or harm the victim and their family. As one victim who testified against her trafficker has said, 'I have moved house three times already, but I still get anonymous phone calls saying, "You owe us. We'll get you." They always know where I am. What can the police do? They do nothing.'

Ways forward

The overarching difficulty with the Belgian and Dutch systems for protection are that they tend to regard the victim in terms of their use as a witness, as a tool for the prosecution of the trafficker, and not as a victim of crime and various human rights violations who has been severely traumatised and is in need of protection and support, regardless of her ability to testify.

There has been an effort to address this in Italy, where residency rights for victims of trafficking are based on the victim's need for social protection rather than on a willingness to testify. Under Italy's revised immigration law (Law 40 of 1998), trafficked persons may get a renewable temporary residence permit for six months if they participate in an assistance and integration programme, regardless of whether they report their trafficker to the authorities. In effect, the implementation still shows a tendency for permits to be granted when victims report their traffickers, but at least it is a step in the right direction by removing the *quid pro quo* of residency in exchange for testimony.

As countries in the European Union and elsewhere adopt and amend laws and policies in order to prosecute traffickers and protect victims more effectively, we need to look closely at what this 'protection' means for trafficked persons. Will it only protect victims in so far as they are co-operative with authorities and testify against their traffickers? How will measures incorporate the specific needs of trafficked women, especially those suffering gender-based violence? How far does participating in the prosecution process empower the victim or further their interests, and how far does it merely expose them and their families to increased danger of reprisals? How can governments protect victims' families in their country of origin? And how can the state continue to protect and support victims in the long term?

We need to address all of these questions if we are to ensure that trafficked persons' human rights are protected and promoted once they are free from their trafficker.

Elaine Pearson is the Trafficking Programme Officer for Anti-Slavery International. She is currently conducting a two-year research study into victim protection measures related to trafficking in ten countries.
E-mail: e.pearson@antislavery.org; http://www.antislavery.org

Notes

1 The term 'trafficked persons' is used throughout this paper to indicate that men, as well as women, are trafficked. However, the vast majority of those who are trafficked are indeed women.

2 This is attached to the United Nations Convention against Transnational Organized Crime. The Trafficking Protocol has been signed by 100 countries to date.

3 Austria and Germany also have similar provisions, but shall not be considered in this paper.

4 For further information on victim protection models, see Berlin State Department of Labour, Vocational Training and Women's Affairs (1998) and Niesner and Jones-Pauly (2001).

References

Advocacy Net (2000) 'Deportation backfires', in *Trafficking in Women: Girls for Sale – Building a Coalition to Fight Trafficking in Nigeria*, http://www.advocacynet.org/cpage_view/nigtraffick_deportation_6_36.html (last checked by author 12 February 2002)

Berlin Senate Department of Labour, Vocational Training and Women's Affairs (1998) 'European Strategies to Prevent and Combat Trafficking in Women', proceedings of an International Conference Commemorating the International Day of Action Against Violence Against Women, 25–6 November, Berlin

Niesner, E. and C. Jones-Pauly (2001) *Trafficking in Women in Europe: Prosecution and Victim Protection in a European Context*, Bielefeld: Kleine Verlag

NGO responses to trafficking in women

Marina Tzvetkova

As trafficking worldwide has become increasingly more sophisticated and widespread, some governments are implementing new legislation, hosting international conferences, and signing new and existing conventions. The United Nations (UN) and other Inter-Governmental Organisations (IGOs) are dedicating substantial resources to developing more effective solutions. However, the relative absence of government initiatives and assistance for trafficking victims, means that it is NGOs who have taken up the challenge of organising locally, nationally, and internationally to advocate for and meet the needs of victims, despite their limited resources. This article provides an overview of NGO activity against trafficking in women for sexual exploitation. It is based on an exploratory study undertaken by the Change Anti-Trafficking Programme (ATP) in 2001. The article explores why NGOs are well-placed to work with women victims of trafficking, and their responses to the growing phenomenon in countries of origin and destination. It presents a regional overview of NGO initiatives, and concludes by discussing some of the main obstacles faced by NGOs in combating trafficking for sexual exploitation, and women's and children's vulnerability to slavery-like practices.

Over the past decade many organisations – governmental, non-governmental and inter-governmental – have launched programmes to address the problem of trafficking of women for sexual exploitation. In order to identify these programmes, in 2001 the Change Anti-Trafficking Programme (ATP) conducted an exploratory study of NGO anti-trafficking activity in countries of origin, transit, and destination. ATP collected and analysed data received from 147 organisations representing 64 countries, in response to a short questionnaire sent to 857 organisations in Asia, Africa, Latin America, Europe, North America, the Middle East, and the Pacific region. The findings are summarised in this article. Analysis of additional information on a further 300 organisations collected through literature reviews, networking, and internet searches is also included.

The scope of NGOs

Despite their limited resources, funding, training, and access to information, most NGOs studied take the lead in combating trafficking in their respective countries. Their anti-trafficking activities, objectives, and orientation are linked to the social and cultural background of their respective countries and regions, and reflect local patterns of trafficking. NGO histories and relationships with governmental institutions vary, as does their scope to contribute to social change and development. For example, most NGOs in Eastern Europe emerged at a time of total social instability in the 1990s, a period characterised by poverty, social change, economic restrictions, inflation, and unemployment. Independent NGO culture was new for peoples who, until then, had been used to totalitarian state structures. Many NGOs faced difficulties dealing with the remains of the outdated and oppressive social system, and the absence of a legislative framework or administrative regulations to legitimise their work. A lack of experienced personnel and limited capacity constituted further challenges, with skills in project management, fundraising, and networking largely absent. These weaknesses and inexperience were manifested at a time when traffickers were becoming increasingly predatory and better at circumventing legal restraints.

A wide range of local, national, and international groups and individuals are involved in anti-trafficking work: women's, human rights, and development organisations, social services and law enforcement agencies, refugee groups, academic institutions, and other professionals. There are varied approaches toward particular problems related to trafficking: different measures and services are required depending on the cultural context, country laws and policies, resources, and the support of local institutions and society.

Why NGOs?

NGOs are often viewed as being the 'conscience of government', and representatives of civil society, and have traditionally stepped in where governments have failed to take the initiative. Trafficking is no exception. NGOs are well-placed to work with trafficked women for several reasons. Many trafficked persons fear and distrust state-based organisations as they frequently enter destination countries illegally, or have had their documentation removed on arrival. Concerns over their immigration status, fear of deportation, and fear of the traffickers, torture, death, and being pressurised to testify translate into mistrust and reluctance to approach statutory agencies for support. Corrupt officials and the involvement of the police and other law enforcement officials can increase distrust.

Many female victims prefer to discuss their situation in a more gender sensitive environment. For this reason, women's NGOs have often been the first line of action – raising awareness, lobbying for change, and providing assistance. It is important to emphasise that NGOs are not a homogeneous group with similar interests. Their diversity is reflected in the interests and issues they promote. Many women's organisations have worked to raise understanding of the importance of gender roles and relations in the national and international arena through their work on issues such as violence against women, promotion and protection of women's human rights worldwide, and women's access to democracy and economic decision-making. Despite the high profile of gender within the development and human rights sectors over the past ten years, not all NGOs are intrinsically gender-sensitive. Some have a more conservative agenda.

Despite cultural, political, and geographical differences, the work and services provided to victims and survivors of trafficking by NGOs have some common features. Support for victims often includes social and psychological assistance, shelter provision, financial, return, and reintegration assistance, telephone advice and counselling, housing, vocational training, legal advice, and documentation assistance.

NGO responses to trafficking in countries of origin

Survivors of trafficking are referred to support services administered by local NGOs on repatriation. NGOs in countries of origin are largely involved in assisting women on their return. They meet them at the airport and provide them with first aid, emergency housing, food and other supplies, medical care, and immediate psychological assistance. In some cases they help women to contact their families, or may contact the families directly. For example, La Strada-Bulgaria sometimes meets parents in advance of a trafficked woman's return to explain the situation, and will pay for parents to come and meet their daughter. NGOs in origin countries have limited capacity to provide all the basic needs of returning trafficked survivors. Therefore, they must work in co-operation with other professionals and organisations. Most NGOs contacted by ATP reported that they had formal or informal referral systems, often based on extensive networking and personal resources. The complex needs and situations of trafficked women require effective, well-established systems of referral.

Few local organisations are able to provide shelter to victims of trafficking (Durand *et al.* 2001). Temporary shelters are often funded by international agencies and administered by local NGOs, but long-term accommodation is seldom available due to insufficient funds and resources. Some shelters are primarily intended for local women survivors of domestic violence, with the places for trafficking victims being exceptional and very limited. Local NGOs resort to emergency accommodation such as renting flats or booking hotels for women to stay in temporarily before they go home to their towns or villages. The need for a long-term solution to the problem of providing safe accommodation for female survivors is crucial, particularly considering the fact that while some women are happy to return to their families, in many cases this is a dangerous or inappropriate solution.

Assistance to trafficked women requires substantial financial resources, and NGOs have limited capacity to offer financial support. In some countries, women cannot access state support and benefits, either because such benefits are unavailable or very limited, or because women are not registered with the social security system. Often, returned survivors of trafficking do not have appropriate documents, or are minors, in which case their parents or family may take responsibility for them, even though their family may have been involved in their trafficking in the first place.

Many trafficked women experience complex post-traumatic stress disorders, and require psychological assistance or hospitalisation. Many of the NGOs identified in our study offer free counselling services or run counselling centres. Counselling centres provide a safe and supportive environment for female survivors where they can share their experiences and receive non-judgemental support and understanding. Work with victims experiencing severe trauma is difficult and requires trained specialists working under close supervision. No survivor of trauma can recover alone (Herman 1994). Organisations that offer psychological counselling to victims often have to deal with the other immediate practical problems that the women may have (such as housing, food, medical assistance, and safety). There is a danger that the continued social and psychological problems experienced by women survivors, if not immediately or adequately tackled by counsellors, will prevent them from trusting service providers and from continuing as clients of the respective service for the time necessary for them to recover.

Legal assistance in countries of origin is essential in cases where women want to instigate legal action against their trafficker. NGOs can offer legal advice and liaise with the respective law enforcement institutions on women's behalf. However there is little that NGOs can do to protect the victim and her family if she decides to testify in court, since witness protection is a prerogative of the state. Very often, traffickers are local people, who know the victim and her family. If the trafficker or their associates are not in detention, there is nothing to prevent them from seeking vengeance.

Re-integration assistance is an area of increasing concern that NGOs cannot approach in isolation. Financial support, community support, and state and institutional support are essential to prevent women from becoming victims again. Without sufficient support for recovery from their traumatic experiences, women face difficulties regaining control over their lives and re-integrating into society. The re-integration process cannot be carried out by a single NGO, although some Eastern European and Asian NGOs put a lot of effort into assisting survivors in this area of work. The reality is that re-integration in countries of origin is confined to a small number of cases. Some rehabilitation programmes are funded by the International Organisation of Migration (IOM) or other international organisations, and implemented by local organisations. Despite these difficulties, some NGOs do assist women. In Asia we have identified small grant programmes for women survivors of trafficking or women and girls at risk. They assist them in developing their own business or continuing their education (Durand *et al.* 2001). In some Eastern European countries, NGOs organise vocational training and other courses for women survivors. Nevertheless, comprehensive re-integration strategies in countries of origin do not exist because of insufficient social security funds and limited resources. Re-integration also requires improving the economic and social conditions of women, and the efforts of various professionals and institutions to this end. In many patriarchal societies, such as Albania, Bangladesh, Iran, and others, it is very difficult for women to re-integrate into their communities, as their options are very limited (Association for Community Development 2001). Community-based approaches to the sensitisation of society to gender and human rights issues therefore become an essential part of the re-integration process.

NGO responses to trafficking in countries of destination

Much of the support for trafficked women in destination countries takes the form of outreach work with sex workers, practical assistance to women who have managed to escape trafficking, and training initiatives for women who have been granted permits to remain.

Shelter in countries of destination is provided to women who have escaped from trafficking situations or who have been rescued by the police and granted temporary residence permits to decide whether to testify against their trafficker. Shelter provision can be controversial. There is a need for a safe place under police protection where women survivors of trafficking can be accommodated. However, women who hold the status of illegal immigrant, or who have been involved in illegal prostitution, will be fearful of coming to a police shelter since they risk detention. Those who wish to escape from prostitution, but do not want to return to their country of origin, cannot benefit from accommodation provision if they hold the status of illegal immigrants. Trafficked women who have decided to continue to work as prostitutes indepen-dent of pimps and brothel owners will be unable to access shelter services. Shelters may also be an inappropriate solution for them.

Social services provided to trafficking victims often include social, psychological, and medical advice and assistance. Again, women can only access these services when they are rescued after police raids or passport checks and referred by the police, or occasionally if they manage to escape from trafficking themselves or with the help of clients.

Outreach work carried out by NGOs in destination countries can be an effective way to reach trafficked women. Illegal immigrants are often not aware that support services are available, or are afraid to seek help. Those kept in isolation or imprisonment are often unable to meet any external contacts apart from their clients and pimps. Many social and medical service providers use outreach workers to talk directly to women on the streets. It can take time for such workers to convince trafficked women that they are not linked to immigration services or the police. Outreach work is usually organised around health education and medical services for women in prostitution. Sometimes information in different languages is circulated so foreign women can find out about the services available. Many organisations employ foreign women as outreach workers or translators. Outreach service providers frequently work to try to empower women who are already in prostitution so that they are able to take care of themselves.

Legal and administrative support is provided by NGOs to help trafficked women to deal with local authorities, immigration, and police. They may support trafficking victims in court, provide legal advice and documentation assistance, and produce and disseminate information on the rights of migrant and trafficked women. Foreign women in destination countries often possess false passports or none at all. They are particularly vulnerable where they do not speak the language of the country, or are not aware of their rights. Even in Italy, the Netherlands, or Germany, where police could help them contact relevant NGOs for assistance, trafficked women are afraid of escaping because they fear detention as illegal migrants, and punishment by the traffickers.

NGO assistance is very much dependent on the national legislation on trafficking and the immigration policies of host countries. Some European countries, such as Germany and the Netherlands, have introduced short stay permits for women who wish to testify against their traffickers in court. However, women often refrain from testifying in court against their traffickers. There are complex reasons for this, including the fear that they or their relatives may be in danger of retaliation attacks. This is reinforced by weak or non-existing witness protection schemes. Current legislation on migration also discourages trafficked women to take the risks of testifying. Often, even survivors who wish to testify find it very difficult to discuss what happened to them. Sometimes it may take considerable time before women are able to talk about their experiences.

In cases where women are granted residence permits, NGOs in co-operation with social services in countries of destination can commence the difficult process of assisting women to integrate into the host community. Common assistance measures include provision of counselling, housing, social and financial support, and vocational and language training. A network of organisations participate in the integration process. Some of them do not work specifically with trafficked women, but assist migrants in general.

For women who wish to return to their home countries, some NGOs in destination countries offer assistance through organising and paying for travel, providing support while a woman is awaiting to being repatriated, liaising with the embassy of her home country, and arranging the necessary travel documents for her. In special cases, representatives of these organisations escort women to their country of origin.

NGOs' role in prevention, lobbying, and research

Many anti-trafficking organisations in origin and destination countries play an important role in research, prevention, advocacy, and awareness-raising. Prevention activities carried out by NGOs include information campaigns, gender education in schools, vocational training for women, training teachers and school advisers to recognise those at risk, and facilitating women at risk to access employment and career development opportunities.

An important component of prevention work in origin countries is the tackling of gender stereotypes, and increasing sensitisation on themes related to violence against women and women's rights. NGOs in destination countries publish educational materials for migrant women, and provide training and technical and financial assistance to their partners from the countries of origin.

International and local NGOs have carried out valuable lobbying and awareness-raising work in bringing trafficking issues to the attention of governments, and advocating for the need to treat trafficking as a human rights violation. Many local and international organisations are active in writing recommendations for legislation and policy developments, and participating in political forums.

Regional overview of NGO responses to trafficking

For ATP's research, organisations in countries of origin, transit, and destination were sent a questionnaire focused around two basic questions about what services were being provided, and which activities developed.

Trafficking in women and girls is widespread and global, but there are different country-specific and regional trends. Eastern Europe is both a region of origin and destination for trafficking, with the Balkans one of the important destination points. Western Europe is the main region of destination for women trafficked from Eastern European countries, Asia (mainly the Philippines and Thailand), Latin America (Brazil, Colombia, and the Dominican Republic), and Africa, particularly West Africa. In East and South-East Asia, the main countries of origin are Thailand, China, the Philippines, Burma/Myanmar, Vietnam, and Cambodia, while Japan is a major country of destination (Human Rights Watch 2000). Asian women are sold to North American brothels, and are trafficked to Australia and increasingly to the Middle East and Gulf States. The following are some of the most interesting findings that emerged from our research.

Asia

In Asia, trafficking in women has been a serious problem for years. Consequently, a wide range of local and international NGOs provide services to Asian trafficking victims.

Most NGOs contacted by ATP were from origin countries. Organisations such as Maiti Nepal, Action Aid India, and Foundation for Women Thailand administer or support rehabilitation centres where women can have access to counselling services, legal and medical assistance, or where referral to these services is available (Durand *et al.* 2001). Asian NGOs also carry out preventative work in their local communities, and initiatives to promote women's and children's rights. Activities include educational programmes for women and girls at risk, vocational training for women, and administration of grants and loans for women who want to start their own businesses.

Maiti Nepal co-ordinates diverse social services for both women and girl victims of trafficking, and potential victims of trafficking. It has three Prevention Camps where children at high risk are given information on what trafficking is. They are trained in different skills for a period of six months, and later provided with micro-funds to ensure sustainability. Maiti Nepal also has transit homes for short stays in the border areas, and a rehabilitation and protection centre which ensures that girls have a safe place to live. They attend a nearby school and return each night to the centre, where there is an emphasis on improving their health and education.

Africa
Despite the seriousness of the problem in Africa, trafficking in women is not recognised as an issue of primary concern amongst the other development problems that Africa faces. Organisations in Africa focus on violence against women, and gender and development. Legal assistance and primary support is provided to women victims of diverse forms of violence including trafficking. African NGOs also undertake public education and awareness campaigns on issues related to trafficking.

Latin America
Latin America was the most difficult region to contact in relation to anti-trafficking initiatives. The main feature of the Latin American NGOs working on trafficking is that they aim at broader issues such as prostitution, and human rights of migrants and children. In fact, most organisations contacted viewed trafficking as a secondary issue related to prostitution, sexual exploitation, or illegal migration. Most NGOs work directly with women – migrants or prostitutes – providing social services, psychological and legal assistance, and counselling.

Western Europe and North America
Western European and North American organisations are more active in research, advocacy, and lobbying. They implement public awareness and advocacy campaigns nationally and sometimes internationally. Many organisations develop strategies for improving and enforcing national and international laws related to trafficking. For this reason, they carry out research on sexual exploitation, and the links between prostitution and trafficking in women and children (Parker 1998; Farley *et al.* 1998). A few organisations work in partnership with NGOs in Asia and Eastern Europe, providing them with technical and financial assistance. They also carry out training initiatives for partners' members and local judiciary and criminal justice systems. The framework of these partnerships is to develop culturally-sensitive responses to the prevention of trafficking or the provision of assistance to trafficked women.

The Pacific
In the Pacific region we had respondents from Australia, the Fiji Islands, the Philippines, and New Zealand. Australia and New Zealand are major destination countries for Asian women. In the Fiji Islands, the Labasa Women's Forum co-ordinates direct services to women as well as developing prevention, education, and awarenessness-raising strategies. The Fiji Women's Rights Movement runs a gender, employment, and economic rights project, which focuses on women migrant workers including trafficking. In the Philippines there is a national alliance of women's organisations called Gabriela. Gabriela is made up of 42,000 members from 250 organisations, institutions, and women's desks or programmes within other institutions. Gabriela launched the *Purple Rose Campaign*, an international campaign against the sex trafficking of Filipino women and children. The campaign is a massive public information and education strategy intended to raise public consciousness of sex-trafficking issues, to provide services to sex-trafficked women, and to organise the survivors.

Middle East
Despite difficulties in eliciting information from the Middle East, ATP discovered that a network to protect trafficking victims is being developed in the region, mainly through voluntary work and without much governmental support. The responses from the Middle East highlight two important

trends in the region. Firstly, the Middle East is a major destination area for trafficked women. Secondly, there is a widespread lack of legal provision to address the issue. This significantly affects the work of local organisations. In this respect, in Israel, research and publications are used in particular to raise awareness about the inadequacy of legal provisions that treat victims of trafficking as 'illegal aliens', and place them in detention (Amnesty International 2000).

Eastern Europe

The diversity of anti-trafficking activities within Eastern Europe is indicative of the extent to which the region is affected by trafficking. Two important areas of work include a wide range of prevention initiatives and work on rehabilitation and re-integration of women survivors of trafficking (La Strada-Czech Republic 2001). The La Strada network, active in eight countries in the region, raises awareness and educates local communities, professional networks, and vulnerable groups of women and girls about the risks of trafficking. La Strada-Poland has produced a video, '*You Have [a] Right to Dream, You Have [a] Right to Know*', which tells the story of a trafficking victim. It was disseminated in several countries and used as a part of lectures in many schools in Poland, Ukraine, and Bulgaria. The International Organisation of Migration (IOM) organised information campaigns in south-eastern Europe. Various projects in Romania, Bulgaria, Kosovo, and Ukraine are being developed to assist rehabilitation of women survivors of trafficking (Reaching Out 2000; Minnesota Advocates for Human Rights 2000; Animus Association 2001).

Conclusion

Our research suggests that much of the anti-trafficking work that addresses the needs of trafficked victims and those at risk is undertaken by NGOs. Governments have tended to focus on introducing and implementing new and existing legislation and hosting conferences. Recently, governments have begun to provide variable amounts of funding for a range of practical anti-trafficking initiatives.

NGOs face considerable barriers in combating trafficking for sexual exploitation. Some of these difficulties arise from the lack of a strong political will to confront and address the problem. Governments, NGOs, police, and law enforcement personnel need to work together to combat trafficking. Government will and effort is integral to addressing both the supply and demand factors that underlie and fuel trafficking.

There is also very little attention paid to gender issues within decision-making processes and with regard to policy formulation and service provision, yet gender inequality is a major factor contributing to the problem of trafficking of women for sexual exploitation. In addition, strong social and cultural constraints mean that addressing unequal gender relations and the social construction of women's roles is difficult. These barriers and constraints severely limit the contributions that NGOs can make to addressing both supply and demand factors of trafficking.

Prevention measures aimed at raising awareness of trafficking, risk recognition, vulnerability avoidance, and support networks are essential components of any anti-trafficking strategy. Long term prevention initiatives require that we confront and address the gender roles and relations that exist (albeit in different forms) in every society and manifest themselves in discriminatory practices and limited opportunities for girls and women at home and the workplace. It means ensuring that women have access to viable economic opportunities as well as political decision making within their countries of origin. Gender analysis in support of prevention would provide a useful approach for tackling trafficking issues.

An additional concern is the inadequate focus placed on the 'demand' side of trafficking for sexual exploitation. Although anti-trafficking experts are divided in their considerations of the harm caused to women by the sex industry, there is a general consensus that the sex industry is expanding rapidly worldwide. Unless there is political will to address the connections between this and trafficking, NGOs can essentially only hope to dress the wound with a sticking plaster.

Marina Tzvetkova is Programme Officer at CHANGE, Anti-Trafficking Programme, Bon Marche Centre, 241-51 Ferndale Road, London SW9 8BJ, United Kingdom.
Tel: +44 (0)20 7733 9928;
E-mail: atp.change@sister.com

References

Amnesty International (2000) *Human Rights Abuses of Women Trafficked from Countries of the Former Soviet Union into Israel's Sex Industry*, London: Amnesty International

Animus Association (2001) *Trafficking in Women: Questions and Answers*, Sofia: Animus Association

Association for Community Development (ACD) (2001) 'Paradigms of Women Trafficking in Bangladesh', Bangladesh: ACD

Durand, T., V. Lattuada, M. Tzvetkova, and A. Plakantonaki (2001) *Anti-Trafficking Programme, Preliminary Study Report*, London: Change

Farley, M., I Baral, M. Kiremire, and U. Sezgun (1998) 'Prostitution in five countries: violence and post-traumatic stress disorder', *Feminism and Psychology* 8(4): 405-26

Herman, J.L. (1994) *Trauma and Recovery, from Domestic Abuse to Political Terror*, London: Pandora

Human Rights Watch (2000) *Owed Justice, Thai Women Trafficked into Debt Bondage in Japan*, New York: Human Rights Watch

La Strada-Czech Republic (2001) *Final Report*, Prague: La Strada

Minnesota Advocates for Human Rights (2000) *Trafficking in Women: Moldova and Ukraine*, Minneapolis: Minnesota Advocates for Human Rights

Parker, J. (1998) *How Prostitution Works*, http://www.prostitutionresearch.com/parker-how.html (last checked by the author October 2001)

Reaching Out (2000) *Annual Activity Report 2000*, Romania: Reaching Out

A tale of two cities:
shifting the paradigm of anti-trafficking programmes

Smarajit Jana, Nandinee Bandyopadhyay, Mrinal Kanti Dutta, and Amitrajit Saha

This article examines the issue of trafficking from the perspective of some sex worker organisations in India and Bangladesh. It argues that inequality between classes, genders, and nations is the root cause of trafficking, and that the solution to the problem lies in a political struggle for the rights of marginalised people. To substantiate these arguments, this article draws on the life stories of trafficked people, and on the preventative anti-trafficking initiatives of sex workers' organisations. In order to understand the ways in which trafficking violates people's rights and restricts their control over their lives we need to focus on the outcomes of trafficking rather than debating the processes through which trafficking takes place. Those who have been trafficked should not be perceived as passive victims of their circumstances, manipulated by others, but as human agents, who can – and often do – fight to gain control over their lives. The article offers a brief introduction and some guidance to some of the challenges that NGOs will face in their advocacy work on trafficking issues.

Over the last decade, the issue of trafficking has dominated international development debates. The ways in which the dominant discourses on trafficking are framed are based on certain assumptions and beliefs which have now come to be taken as the 'truth', without being challenged. These discourses usually define trafficking as a process where a person loses control over their own life; they equate sex work to trafficking, and stress the restriction of movement of weaker and vulnerable sections of society. Police rescue and so-called 'rehabilitation' initiatives become the cornerstone of most of the programmes arising out of this thinking. At international conferences on trafficking, as well as in the popular media, those who are involved in anti-trafficking efforts contend tenaciously that the trafficking of people across international borders has escalated dramatically in the last decade. Equally, it is asserted that the funding of activities to curb trafficking has also grown exponentially. If we stop to ponder for a minute, it is clear that for both postulations to be true at the same time, something must be wrong. Either the definitions or perceptions of trafficking and the estimates of its volume must be mistaken, or the types of anti-trafficking initiatives intended to address it have been ineffective. In this article we present our own understanding of this issue, based on our experiences of working with sex workers' organisations running anti-trafficking programmes.

Redefining trafficking

In order to have an impact on trafficking we need to focus on two courses of action, namely, exploring the root causes of trafficking, and recognising the positive role of human agency. Durbar Mahila Samanwaya Committee (DMSC) in Kolkata, one of the largest organised groups for sex workers, defines trafficking as an outcome of a process where:

- people are recruited and moved within or across national borders without informed consent, and coerced into a 'job' or occupation against their will;
- the trafficked individual loses control over his/her occupation and life.

People have always left home in search of new lives, better livelihoods, or simply to seek adventure. Traditionally, women often had to hold back on exploring alternatives because of rigid gender norms and lack of opportunities. As a result of globalisation, the realignment of social and cultural relations, and radical changes in the labour market, mean that more and more women, who were traditionally confined to the home, are now seeking alternative, preferred, and more viable livelihood options elsewhere.

DMSC sees this as a positive and potentially revolutionary development, creating a window of opportunity to challenge existing gender and class inequalities. However, existing political systems, combined with increasingly stringent anti-immigration national laws in most countries, make such migration hazardous, particularly for poor or marginalised aspiring migrants who are vulnerable to being smuggled illegally into the countries they seek to enter. As long as the current economic globalisation process privileges movement of finance capital while restricting the movement of labour or human capital across national borders, trafficking of people will continue.

Women, men, and children are trafficked for various purposes, such as marriage, agricultural labour, working in various informal sector industries, domestic labour, participating in dangerous sports such as camel racing, recruitment in armed conflict, and for sex work.

The most critical element of trafficking is not necessarily the process through which a person is trafficked, nor the nature of the job or practices for which the person is trafficked: rather, it is the outcome of that process that is instrumental in leaving the trafficked person with little or no option to leave the place or position in which they find themselves. Trafficked persons are recruited into various jobs, for which they can be made to work without the wages or the minimum benefits that have to be provided to regular members of the labour force. If the entire employment market, in both formal and unorganised sectors, could be regulated in adherence to national and international labour laws protecting the rights of workers, and if all workers were conscious of their labour rights, were organised, and had a role in regulating the workplace, the demand for trafficked labour would cease to exist.

Patriarchal legislation and controls

Recently, in countries across the world, more and more stringent laws have been introduced to curb trafficking in order to protect women. In effect, these laws restrict the free movement of women. Bangladesh, which is one of the major labour exporting countries of South Asia, has enacted a law preventing single women from travelling across its borders. Not only do such laws violate the fundamental human right to mobility, and discriminate against women, they also exacerbate the vulnerability of women to being trafficked: where no legal options are available to them, they must depend on the illicit options offered by traffickers. Special booths have been set up by the state in collaboration with NGOs at the borders where women crossing the frontier are interrogated in order to verify their identity and to judge whether they may be allowed to continue (CARE 2001a).

It is often argued, in several forums, that restricting movement across borders, through new legislation or more stringent implementation of existing laws, prevents trafficking. In fact, these kinds of restrictions can work to strengthen the influence of organised crime. The prime motivating factor that impels people to move from villages to cities and from one country to another is their aspiration to improve their life conditions, a basic social instinct that has always shaped human civilisation. If people cannot migrate legally, they will resort to illegal mechanisms. Only large, organised criminal networks have the resources and wherewithal to bypass strict state control at international borders. This in turn leads to the development of ever larger crime syndicates, as has happened in Eastern Europe.

Stricter border control also increases the risks for those who are trafficked, as traffickers choose increasingly hazardous routes and methods to escape detection. Moreover, such controls expose women to greater exploitation because of existing gender inequalities and social vulnerabilities.

Only global structural political and economic changes can create a new scenario where trafficking becomes redundant. For example, unrestricted movement of labour across international borders would mean that a poor Third World woman could travel legitimately to a First World market to seek employment, just as her richer and more qualified counter-part is able to. Access to legitimate avenues of migration would reduce the risk of being entrapped by a trafficker. Universal education and equal access to information would also reduce the risk of potential migrants being deceived by traffickers.

When it comes to dealing with those who have already been trafficked, no attempt has been made to implement a set of standard rules, code of conduct, or self-imposed norms by the NGOs or state agencies who implement rescue and rehabilitation programmes. Nor has any effort been made to enable the participation of those trafficked in designing a programme of rehabilitation.

It is very critical that we look into the issue of participation in this regard. That the direct participation of those who are trafficked in preventing and ameliorating the effects of trafficking is both ethical and effective has been demonstrated by the experiences of the Durbar Mahila Samanwaya Committee (DMSC) in this regard (Durbar Mahila Samanwaya Committee 1998, 1999, 2001). Moreover, DMSC's expertise, based on its achievements in the last couple of years, has already been transferred to other sex worker organisations in Bangladesh.

Tales from two cities: the realities of trafficking and anti-trafficking work

The following stories demonstrate the different realities of women trafficked into sex work. The reasons why many women and girls are trafficked into prostitution include a combination of individualised choices to improve their situation through seeking better lives and employment opportunities in cities and other countries. These choices are not afforded to them within their own setting due to poverty, discrimination, inequality, and in some cases, gender-based violence.

Farzana's story: seeking a better life

Farzana left her village in 1997, determined to find new opportunities and a better life. She stayed with a friend in a city slum, who, after a couple of weeks, found her a job in a garment factory. Within a couple of months her supervisor started paying her unwelcome attention and finally proposed to her. She did not like him, so she refused. The supervisor sacked her. The sense of liberty and freedom that she had now experienced, especially in contrast with the life she had led before coming to Dhaka and working, stopped Farzana from going back to her village. She was determined to find something better.

She got an offer to work in the neighbouring town of Narayanganj and took it up. However, she found herself trafficked into a brothel in Tanbazar.[1] She tried to run away but was unsuccessful, and continued to work as a bonded labourer. After a year she paid off her debt to the brothel owner and was free to leave. At this juncture she pondered over what to do next. Eventually she decided to continue in the sex trade, as many others do.

In the middle of one night in 1999, policemen broke open the door of Farzana's room in the brothel and kicked her out. Along with many other sex workers, she was pushed into a police van and taken to a remand home. At the remand home she was persistently abused, physically and sexually. Her only hope for getting out of the remand home was to accept the rehabilitation programme offered by the government. This rehabilitation package included 5000 *taka* in cash and a sewing machine. Farzana was told that if she did not accept the deal she would have to remain in the home forever. She agreed, but then the authorities stipulated that unless her parents came to take custody of her, Farzana would not be allowed to leave the home.

There was no way Farzana could get in touch with her parents and persuade them to come and 'rescue' her. By this time, however, Farzana had learnt that there were people who would pose as her parents in exchange for 4500 of the 5000 *taka*, and the sewing machine. Farzana came out of the home with many others. Having lost all her savings at the time of the eviction, all she had with her was 500 *taka*. With 500 *taka* in her pocket and no place to live, she had no other option but to take to the streets or try and find another job in the garments industry.

The role of human agency: Farzana's aspirations, choices, and risks

Farzana's story raises a number of issues. When Farzana left for Dhaka, it was not mere poverty that drove her. She risked venturing out into the unknown because she could no longer accept the circumstances under which she was forced to live at home. As soon as she had reached puberty she was withdrawn from school. She was not even allowed to study at home since her father had decided it would be a bad investment, as she would eventually marry into another family. She was not allowed to play with her friends in the fields any longer. All she did was work at home from dawn until dusk performing repetitive, mind-numbing, and unending household chores. This work would never teach her skills that could earn her a living. It was her aspiration to break free of the boundaries imposed on her as an adolescent Muslim girl in a Bangladeshi village, and her determination to get more out of life, that brought Farzana to the city. The fact that someone who was not allowed to leave home could make such a life-changing move represents a triumph of human agency. The question we have to confront now is: how far are we ready to acknowledge and respect Farzana's human agency, and accept her right to find her own destiny?

In the city, Farzana found a job. For the first time in her life she was independent. She acquired new skills and earned money over which she had control. With her co-workers she could walk in the city streets whenever she wanted. However, when she decided to extend her new-found autonomy to thwart the designs of her supervisor, she lost her job.

Farzana could have returned home at this point. But knowing what awaited her there, she did not want to forego her hard-earned freedom. So she desperately looked for another job. It was at this juncture that she was trafficked. An agent who had promised to find her another job sold her to a brothel owner, making a tidy profit. The brothel owner too made money out of Farzana's vulnerability by making her work without wages until she had made substantial profits over and above the money she had invested in procuring Farzana.

Until the brothel owner was satisfied with her profit, Farzana was bonded and could not opt out of the condition she found herself in, however much she wanted to. It is to be noted that after overcoming the constraints imposed on her by social conditions against all odds on two earlier instances, Farzana, not having any resource other than her own free will and determination, could no longer surmount the material boundaries of her situation.

However, the period of bondage came to an end after one year. Once again, Farzana was at a crossroads. She had to decide whether to continue working in the sex trade or to take her chances in other job markets. Considering all her options, Farzana decided to continue to work as a sex worker. At this point, Farzana had some control over her working conditions and was free to leave the trade whenever she wanted.

What needs to be understood is that even in such adversity, Farzana managed to escape from her trafficked conditions. At this point she can no longer be considered to be 'in a trafficked situation'. It is to be noted that all trafficking situations are time-bound and usually do not extend throughout someone's entire life, or inter-generationally. This has significant implications for future anti-trafficking approaches and strategies .

Farzana's experience of forced rehabilitation

Government policy to evict all sex workers and place them in a remand home put paid to Farzana's prospects. In violation of her fundamental rights, she was forcibly evicted from her home and workplace. She was insulted and physically abused. She was then imprisoned in a remand home, once again finding herself in a situation over which she had no control. In addition, she was sexually exploited and abused at the remand home while under the supposed protection of the state. Farzana now found herself in a situation no different from the one under which she lived when she was trafficked. This raises the question of whether forced 'rehabilitation' ought to be seen as trafficking too.

The government then unilaterally decided on a rehabilitation deal for imprisoned sex workers. None of the sex workers were consulted about what they wanted, completely disregarding their agency. Secondly, they were offered no choice in the matter: they were told that if they did not accept the government package they would have to resign themselves to life-long imprisonment. The government then imposed the additional condition that the rehabilitation package would be handed over to the sex workers only with their parents' authorisation. This infantilised the sex workers, and created the conditions for further exploitation. The entire exercise clearly demonstrates how any scheme that is designed with no consultation with the intended users can be counter-productive.

Who is to blame?

Farzana found herself on the streets again, exposed to greater vulnerability than before. We must ask ourselves, is it not the lack of appropriate work environment and conditions in formal and informal sectors, such as the garments industry and the sex trade, that facilitates perpetual exploitation of the most vulnerable groups? Had there been proper protection of labour rights in the garments industry, Farzana would not have been sacked at the whim of her supervisor in the first place. Had there been adequate trade regulations within the sex industry, Farzana or any other sex worker would not have been made to work without wages, nor would any brothel owner be allowed to employ trafficked labour. In such a case, the need for trafficking would not have arisen, as there would have been no extra gains to be made from recruiting trafficked persons. The issue here is, what role did the state play – or fail to play – in safeguarding workers' rights and securing workplace safety to prevent extreme forms of exploitation of workers such as Farzana? Is providing workers with some control over their occupation a more appropriate or effective strategy for governments?

Sofia's story: dealing with HIV

Sofia, a friend of Farzana's who had also been evicted from Tanbazar and later remanded at the same home, decided to opt out of the sex trade. She took the help of an NGO to seek an alternative livelihood. The NGO put her in a shelter home. Immediately on her arrival, the NGO personnel took a sample of her blood, and tested it for HIV without her knowledge or consent. She was found to be HIV positive. The NGO personnel informed her of this, and very quickly, all the staff members of the shelter home came to know her status. The rules of the shelter home were that no rescued women were allowed to meet and communicate with outsiders without prior permission from the official in charge of the shelter home, and that communication could only take place at fixed hours in a month. This lack of communication meant that nobody outside of the home knew what was happening to Sofia. After a couple of weeks, Farzana heard that Sofia had committed suicide. Her body was not even sent for a post mortem examination, a common practice internationally following any unnatural death (Mondol 2001).

Monica's story: choosing to go back

Monica had come to Dhaka from Satkhira with her father and younger brother. Her father and brother worked on a construction site, and Monica found a job in a small shop close to the site. They found out that across the border in Barasat the wage rates for construction work were higher, and the working hours were shorter. The next season, they paid an agent to help them cross the border to Barasat in India without legitimate papers in order to find work on a construction site. Monica heard from other female workers that wages in Kolkata were even higher so she started looking for ways to find work there. One morning, Monica's father found that she had gone.

After nine months Monica came back to Satkhira bringing gifts and 5000 *taka*. She had been trafficked and sold into the sex industry, where she had worked for four months bonded to the brothel owner who had bought her. Once the bondage term was over, she stayed on in the trade working for another brothel owner and sharing her earnings with her. Initially, her family and neighbours seemed appalled by the fact that she had 'fallen' into prostitution. The local religious leader arbitrated that Monica would have to pay a fine of 150 *taka* to seek re-entry into the community. Once she paid this amount, the rest of the members of the community accepted Monica back.

Gradually, Monica came to know that many women from her locality had gone through the same process, through which they managed to accumulate considerable wealth and improve their living conditions. From her savings, Monica bought a piece of land and met the costs of her mother's treatment for a long-term illness. Now Monica is preparing to go back to Kolkata to work in the sex industry for a few years so that she can support her parents and also save for her future. She is looking for an agent who will take her across the border for a fee.

A survey conducted by CARE showed that, like Monica, 22 per cent of women who have experienced trafficking actually choose to return to the occupation into which they were trafficked (CARE 2001c).

Why is Monica not afraid of being trafficked again? Quite rightly, Monica has identified the real reason for her vulnerability to being trafficked. It was her lack of knowledge that made her susceptible to being deceived and trafficked. Now that she knows how the sex industry works and has control over the capital she has, she is confident that she can determine the terms under which she works. If women at risk of being trafficked were provided with information of how the market works, and were guaranteed control over their working conditions, the possibility of being trafficked into slavery-like conditions would be hugely reduced.

There are hundreds of Farzanas, Sofias, and Monicas, all of whom could tell a similar story, if we would only stop to ask them. In the course of our work in Dhaka and Kolkata, the numerous Farzanas, Sofias, and Monicas have recounted these experiences to us. To us these narratives raise a number of important questions. Should we address the process or the outcome of trafficking? Should we be shocked and horrified by these stories or concerned with the interests, opinions, and life-strategies of those trafficked? If the basic objective of our anti-trafficking efforts is to enhance the well-being of the individual and help improve her livelihood options, then the role of that individual and that of other third parties involved in the individual's rescue and rehabilitation should come under thorough scrutiny. The processes of deceit, coercion, and exploitation, which define trafficking, are not perpetrated by traffickers alone; in the name of rescue and rehabilitation, agents of the state and private actors may also employ such tactics. There is no code of conduct followed by all these agencies to ensure the protection of the rights and dignity of the victims while carrying out their work. NGOs participating in a consultative meeting recently held in Dhaka strongly recommended the development and inclusion of codes of conduct while dealing with anti- trafficking programmes (CARE 2001b).

DMSC's programme approach

Following our principle objective to dissociate sex work from all criminal associations, DMSC entered into the arena of anti-trafficking activities in 1998, and quickly developed a strategy to stop the trafficking of women and children into sex work in Kolkata. DMSC sees sex work as a contractual service, negotiated between consenting adults. In such a service contract there ought to be no coercion or deception. As a sex workers' rights organisation, DMSC is against any force exercised against sex workers, be it by the client, brothel keepers, room owners, pimps, police, or traffickers.

DMSC's programme approach is very simple. Members of DMSC keep a strong vigil in the red light districts through a group of volunteers who intercept any new entrants into the area, make enquiries about where they have come from and their relationship with the people accompanying them, if any, and thoroughly examine the role of brothel owners and landlords in the process of their recruitment. They can effectively stop the entry of any under-age woman, or women who are being coerced into the trade. They do this in two ways. Firstly, being in the trade themselves they are able to identify cases of trafficking much more easily than an outsider could. Secondly, as members of a very organised labour force in the city, they can exert their power to remove or 'rescue' such women from the clutches of any unscrupulous brothel owners and pimps who have procured them. In most cases, trafficked women are counselled and sent back to their homes or to boarding schools (when the person is a minor) with the help of the Ministry of Social Welfare, but without involving the law enforcing authorities in general.

The process is not as simple as it appears to be. Contrary to popular belief, the people who usually challenge or resist DMSC's anti-trafficking interventions are not the traffickers, or others with a stake in the sex industry. It is the state and its law enforcing authorities who create the greatest barrier.

Madhabi's story: 'sacrifice a life' or obey the law of the land?

As a teenager, Madhabi had fallen in love with a distant relative, Mukul. Her parents did not endorse Madhabi's love affair. When her parents insisted that she end her relationship with Mukul and marry a man they had chosen for her, Madhabi ran away from home with Mukul. They rented a room in the suburbs of Kolkata and started living together. Mukul had neither income nor the skills to find any job in the city. They managed to survive during the first couple of months by selling Madhabi's jewellery.

One morning, Mukul left home in search of a job and did not return. Two days later Mukul's friends turned up saying they had come to take Madhabi to a hospital where Mukul had been admitted following a serious accident. Travelling for more than an hour by bus and tram, they arrived at a place that Madhabi did not recognise. Confused, she found herself in an unfamiliar street. 'How could it be a hospital?', she mumbled. She had never seen so many women standing in the street, talking so loudly.

As she hesitated, Mukul's friends dragged her to the staircase of the nearby building. At that very moment they heard a harsh voice from behind asking them to stop. Unknown to Mukul's friends DMSC volunteers had followed them since their arrival into the red light area, finding their movements to be suspicious.

Madhabi was brought to the DMSC office for counselling and other support. The other volunteers found Mukul lurking in the brothel Madhabi was being taken to, and took him and his friends to the local police station. After a brief dialogue, the officer in charge asked DMSC members to hand Mukul and Madhabi over in order to register a case of trafficking against Mukul. The officer argued that without taking custody of Madhabi, who was purportedly being trafficked, no case could be booked against Mukul. The volunteers returned to the DMSC office. A debate soon ensued, with other members of DMSC joining in, which continued for a couple of hours without reaching any conclusion.

What was being debated was Madhabi's fate. Should she be handed over to the police in order that Mukul would be punished, or should she be allowed to follow a course of action of her own choice? DMSC members knew that putting Madhabi in police custody could mean indirectly 'forcing' her into the sex trade, which she did not want to engage in. Usually when a trafficked woman is rescued from the sex trade and put into police custody, the police accommodate her in the government remand home, which is notorious for corruption and for unofficial linkages with the trafficking racket.

In DMSC's experience, the brothel owners who recruit trafficked women have a system worked out by which they can pay a bribe to the remand home authorities in order to have the woman returned to them. They then extract the amount they had invested – often inflating it considerably – from the trafficked woman by making her work without wages. Moreover, the process through which Madhabi would have to pass once put in the hands of the law enforcement system, from police custody, to judicial custody, to remand home, is both lengthy and hazardous. The police and the caretakers of the remand home, are likely to treat her with no dignity, and may sexually abuse her.[2]

At the end of such a process, her already restricted options would be reduced to none whatsoever.

None of the representatives of the DMSC were inclined to hand Madhabi over to the police. On the other hand, not doing so would result in the traffickers going unpunished. This posed the biggest dilemma to the members of the organisation. Their accumulated experience over the period had shown them that they would have to follow one or other of the two possible courses of action. One is to obey the norms and rules of the state. The other is to respect Madhabi's wishes and take a stand outside the law so as to reverse the outcome of trafficking for her, and enhance her options to improve her life chances. Most DMSC members opted for the second path.

Sex workers' organisation and action

During the last two years, DMSC has recovered 47 trafficked women, of whom 35 were minors, and taken them to safe custody. We have repatriated four minors from Bangladesh and two from Nepal, and have helped 12 Indian minors to return home.

DMSC runs a primary prevention programme providing alternative livelihood training to those who do not want to continue in sex work, as part of its broader aim to respect the choices of individuals. Training has been provided to 112 adolescents and 32 adults in skills such as silk-screen printing, toy making, and clay modelling. In addition to reducing young adults' vulnerability to sex work, DMSC has in the last year recruited 25 daughters of sex workers as teachers on their ongoing education programme for sex workers and their children. They are provided with on-the-job training, which they may later use to seek alternative employment.

DMSC has reduced the economic vulnerability of sex workers and their children by running a savings and credit programme through the sex workers' co-operative institution, Usha Multipurpose Co-operative Society Limited. It has a membership of about 3500, representing different brothels in Kolkata.

DMSC also trains sex workers from neighbouring countries in order to make cross-border anti-trafficking efforts more effective. It acts in close collaboration with sex workers' organisations and supporting NGOs in Bangladesh and Nepal, particularly in the repatriation of trafficked persons.

Challenges

DMSC has faced some major challenges[3], including strong opposition from law-enforcing authorities who criticise DMSC for taking the law into its own hands and violating the constitutional boundaries between the state and civil society. Although DMSC succeeded in creating a support base within local police institutions, without which they could not have carried out their anti-trafficking activities at the field level, contradictions with the legal and judicial system remain. This poses a constant threat to DMSC's intervention in this arena, as its extra-constitutional role can be used against it.

The broader political context, which extends beyond the red light districts but profits from the exploitation and trafficking of sex workers within the sex industry, has started attempting, in various guises, to oppose DMSC's efforts to stop trafficking into the sex trade.

The prevalent positions and practices of NGOs, both local and international, also pose a challenge to sex workers' interventions in trafficking. This conflict is on the one hand an ideological one. Sex workers and trafficked persons who take the initiative to deal with their own problems as actors in development, rather than passive recipients, are challenging the conventional role of NGOs and the enlightened middle classes working on behalf of the poor. On the other hand, there is an immediate conflict of interest. If more and more sex workers' organisations gain the capacity and the confidence to implement intervention activities themselves, NGOs will become apprehensive that their role as mediator will gradually become redundant.

In fact, sex workers' and trafficked persons' demands for the right to self-determination and autonomy represent an ideological challenge not just to the prevalent development practices by NGOs, but to all discourses that reduce marginalised people, particularly women, to being submissive victims of their circumstance, devoid of human agency, and unable to steer their own destiny unless 'rescued' through the benevolence of others.

Self-regulatory boards: a way forward

To overcome all these challenges, DMSC has been institutionalising the process of their anti-trafficking interventions through establishing self-regulatory boards. DMSC has so far established three local self-regulatory boards in Kolkata, and is in the process of setting up similar boards in all red light areas. Sixty percent of the members of these boards are sex workers, and the rest are comprised of local elected representatives of the people, representatives of the state, legal professionals, and medical doctors.

The primary objectives of these boards are to prevent exploitation and violation of human rights within the sex trade; to initiate comprehensive development programmes for the sex workers' community; and to ensure the community's right to self-determination. The boards are involved in various programmes such as mitigating violence against sex workers; establishing channels of information within the red light area through which the board members can monitor whether any children are being trafficked into sex work or whether anyone is being made to work against her will; identifying those who have been trafficked, and encouraging them to seek the help of the self-regulatory board; trauma counselling of those recovered, and providing them with health services if required; repatriation of those who are recovered, with representatives of the boards accompanying them; establishing ways of keeping in touch with those who are repatriated, with the help of collaborative sex workers' organisations and NGOs in their native countries, to ensure that they are not stigmatised or re-trafficked.

It seems to us that this unique approach can open up new ways of designing and implementing anti-trafficking programmes, and can help us to think through and reframe the development discourse and practice on anti-trafficking programmes globally.

Smarajit Jana is Programme Co-ordinator, HIV Programme, CARE-Bangladesh, and Chief Adviser for Durbar. 59, 7A Dhanmondi, Dhaka 1209, Bangladesh. Tel: +880 2 882 4974; +880 2 811 4195-97;
E-mail: carehiv@bangla.net;
jana@carebangladesh.org

Nandinee Bandyopadhyay is a consultant in gender, politics, and organisations, and an adviser for Durbar. Flat 4C, 146 Rash Behari Avenue, Kolkata 700 029, India.
Tel: +91 33 543 7777; +91 33 543 7560;
E-mail: nandineeb@satyam.net.in

Mrinal Kanti Dutta is Programme Director at Durbar, 12/5 Nilmani Mitra Street, Kolkata 700 006, India. Tel: +91 33 543 7560;
E-mail: durbarmahila@vsnl.net

Amitrajit Saha works for the National Polio Surveillance Programme, India, and is an Adviser for Durbar. Flat 4C, 146 Rash Behari Avenue, Kolkata 700 029, India.
Tel: +91 6456 23 390; +91 6456 24 331;
E-mail: ship@cal.vsnl.net.in

Notes

1 Tanbazar was the largest functioning brothel in Bangladesh, till July 1999. In the middle of the night, the Law Enforcing Department organised a brutal 'raid' and evicted all inhabitants of the brothel, some 4500 sex workers. The incident was widely covered in local newspapers.

2 Focus group discussion with DMSC members, held in their Kolkata office, 26 November 2001.

3 Interview with Angura Begum, Secretary, DMSC, Kolkata, 27 November 2001.

References

CARE (2001a) Proceedings of a workshop on 'Cross-border Trafficking Prevention', organised by CARE Bangladesh in Dhaka, October 17-18 2001, Dhaka: Care Bangladesh

CARE (2001b) Minutes of a consultative meeting organised by CARE Bangladesh, Dhaka, 10 September 2001, Dhaka: Care Bangladesh

CARE (2001c) 'Report of Ethnographic Study', unpublished report of the Anti-trafficking Project of CARE-Bangladesh, Dhaka: Care Bangladesh

Durbar Mahila Samanwaya Committee (DMSC) (1998) 'Seven Years Stint at Sonagachi: DMSC, Human Development, and Social Action', Kolkata: DMSC

Durbar Mahila Samanwaya Committee (DMSC) (1999) 'Second State Conference of the Sex Workers Report: 30th April to 1st May 1999', DMSC: Kolkata

Durbar Mahila Samanwaya Committee (DMSC) (2001) 'Millennium Milan Mela', Kolkata: DMSC

Mondol, P. (2001) 'HIV, Death and Justice: The Dhaka Experience', poster presented at the 6th ICAAP conference held in Melbourne, October 2001

Reducing poverty and upholding human rights:
a pragmatic approach

Meena Poudel and Ines Smyth

Trafficking in women is increasing in many countries around the world. This global problem is now well recognised by policy makers and aid agencies committed to poverty reduction in all its forms. This paper considers how Oxfam GB perceives the problem of trafficking of women in the context of its approach to poverty. It illustrates this position through a case study of a young woman whose human rights were violated through the process of trafficking, and provides examples of projects and programs implemented in various regions of the world to address to the underlying causes. Oxfam's broad trafficking programme objectives are: to promote the fundamental rights of women; to protect potential victims and survivors of trafficking; to influence national policies, and regional and international conventions on women's rights and trafficking.

The key argument of this paper is that Oxfam recognises that debates[1] around the interpretations of what trafficking is are important as they influence the kind of policies implemented to eradicate the problem and support the victims. However, Oxfam adopts a principled but pragmatic approach to the issue. Pragmatic in that it looks at the problem within its socio-economic context. Principled in that it bases work in this field on Oxfam's understanding of poverty as a denial of the basic rights to which every human being is entitled, and on its perception that poverty is of different kinds, all of which need to be understood and eradicated.

Oxfam GB: poverty, rights, and the trafficking of women

Oxfam GB's mandate is to overcome poverty and suffering. In carrying out this mandate, the organisation relies on a basic understanding of poverty which stresses that:

> *'All people are entitled to the rights enshrined in international laws and conventions: social and economic rights, civil and political rights, and the right to life itself, free from fear and persecution. But many people are denied these rights as a consequence of neglect or oppression. Denying people their rights forces them into poverty and keeps them there.'*
> (Oxfam 2002)

In order to maximise its resources and achieve 'maximum impact', Oxfam focuses its policy and programme work on five key aims:

- the right to a sustainable livelihood;
- the right to health and education;
- the right to life and security;
- the right to be heard;
- the right to equity: gender and diversity.

A concern about the denial of human rights inherent in trafficking fits well within Oxfam's overall understanding of poverty and rights. In addition, Oxfam has prioritised certain areas of work and initiated specific interventions within a global programme to end violence against women, including that against trafficked women and girls within its fifth aim (the right to equity). There is also a commitment to work towards 'getting institutions right for women and overcoming discrimination', through which Oxfam tries to reach the institutional roots of biases in policies and practices that discriminate against women and against women, men, and children on the basis of their racial, ethnic, or other identity.

The case of Niru,[2] a Nepali woman, helps demonstrate the violence, human rights violations, and gender discrimination that characterise trafficking in women, as well as the role of social institutions such as the family, household, community, labour market, sex industry, and the state in perpetuating this.

'A recruitment agent came to my village offering jobs and my parents agreed to send my brother and me. Both of us agreed because we needed money to pay back our loan. I came to Kathmandu when I was 12 years [old] *to work in a garment factory. I worked there for a year then a recruiting manager offered me another job in India where I could get more money. They took five girls including me to India by public bus. They asked us to stay in a room with a woman and promised to bring us food. They never came back.*

I found myself in a brothel. I had been sold for 50,000 Nepalese rupees [US$700]. *I had to satisfy five to eight clients per night but I did not get any money – only two meals a day. I spent seven years there and tried to escape three times but didn't succeed. During that time I could not contact my family.*

We were 20 girls staying in the same room. There were few rooms set aside for each girl to serve clients for sex. During my menstruation period the owner used to inject drugs into my thigh before [I went] *with* [a] *client. Initially I had tuberculosis but later I was diagnosed as HIV positive.*

One day the police raided that brothel and I managed to escape. I stayed in the Indian Government Observation Home for six months. I was taking medicine for tuberculosis but I could not continue my medication because I had no money and the observation did not provide me with any. In the end I managed to get back home with all problems but no money.

When I went back home I found out that my mother had died a year ago. My father loved me but my village refused to accept me because I was considered a bad woman. Village leaders threatened my father that he had to leave the village if he accepted me. I returned to Kathmandu and joined a group of survivors of trafficking. Now I am involved in an anti-trafficking project that raises awareness of trafficking and the consequences to my Nepali sisters. I know I cannot change my life but I have hope that I can make a contribution to society through Shakti Shamuha[3] to providing information about the dangers to my sisters who are vulnerable to this crime. My biggest frustration is that I cannot get a citizenship certificate because of the social rejection, patriarchal society, and my father being prevented from recommending me for citizenship. My father's permission is an essential requirement. Because of my position I cannot take up invitations from abroad to visit and establish links with other campaigns against trafficking. To me there is no country, no system that can protect my rights, and there is no society where I belong. Where are my rights?

The example is a useful illustration of how human rights can be violated in all three stages of trafficking: recruitment, work, and rescue.

Recruitment

In a typical situation, a woman or girl is recruited by an agent with promises of a good or better job in another province or country, with false documents supplied, if required. In extreme cases, girls and women are abducted. Once recruited or abducted, many women and girls are forced into sex work or controlled through debt bondage. Thereafter, threats and use of violence, coercion, and torture are not uncommon. Basic needs such as food, medicine, rest, and safe shelter can also be denied to the victim.

Abuse of authority by officials within state institutions is another form of violence that trafficked women face, as is the violation of their rights to freedom, movement, and information during transit. There is ample evidence that corrupt officials within the police and immigration services often exacerbate the experience of those who are trafficked (Asia Watch 1993). Countries can also benefit from tourism (including sex tourism) and, in the case of other forms of forced labour, from the avoidance of paying welfare benefits. They are therefore less likely to take a strong anti-trafficking position.

Work

Niru's case illustrates some of the human rights violations within a work environment. These include violation of contracts, unpaid labour, unsafe working conditions, lack of safe drinking water, lack of safe and sufficient food, unlimited time of work, underpayment, and no right to formal unionised labour. Debt bondage is key to the conditions of dependency and slavery in which trafficked women and children live. Other violations include denial of access to health services, forced use of drugs, and exposure to sexually transmitted diseases including HIV/AIDS.

Rescue

Human rights may also be violated at the rescue stage of the trafficking process. Oxfam GB's experience of working with trafficked survivors and campaigners in Nepal shows that often the rescue of Nepali women in Nepal and in India gives cause for concern. Survivors may be illegally arrested by police and detained, and even raped and abused in custody. They are also subjected to forced medical check-ups and treatments, particularly HIV testing. The legal process is equally arbitrary and abusive. Women are forced to testify in public in long and demanding legal proceedings, with no access to independent lawyers. They are often humiliated in court or deported without due process. This violates human rights principles such as freedom from torture and arbitrary arrest and detention, and the right to protection, liberty, security, privacy, and a fair and speedy trial.

Niru's case also illustrates the discriminatory role of social institutions. Denial of citizenship and rejection by the community not only prevent women such as Niru from taking advantage of limited opportunities for solidarity and for improvements in their lives, but also raise fundamental questions about the limited rights that women may access as citizens, both in countries of origin and destination.

Working against the trafficking of women

The realities of trafficked women and girls differ according to country-specific contexts, reflecting the multi-faceted causes and consequences of trafficking. Oxfam's engagement with the problem also varies in different countries and regions, reflecting the priorities of partner organisations. The size of the programme and types of activities undertaken depend on a variety of factors: country and regional priorities identified by partners and staff; access to necessary resources; and the historical evolution of individual programmes.

With the exception of small-scale project work in the former Yugoslavia and in Latin America, most of Oxfam's work on trafficking takes place in Asia. In the UK, Oxfam also provides support to the Refugee Council (of which Oxfam is a founding member), particularly for information and advocacy work on international refugee and asylum issues. One example of this support is a project Oxfam funded in 1998 for research into trafficking and smuggling of refugees, called 'The Cost of Survival'. In addition, a joint Oxfam GB and NOVIB (Oxfam in the Netherlands) project supports research into best practice on the integration and re-integration of women who are victims of trafficking, through a UK-based organisation and a Dutch NGO.

Most anti-trafficking activities are carried out through partner organisations and networks, rather than by Oxfam directly. For example, in Cambodia, Oxfam supports, among other national agencies, KWVC and ADHOC. KWVC is an organisation that works to promote women's participation and decision-making in politics, society, and economics. It aims to eliminate discrimination against women and promote laws to protect women's rights. ADHOC is a local human rights and development organisation that plays a significant role in rights education, monitoring, advocacy, and lobbying. Both have programmes that raise awareness of women's and children's rights on issues like sex trafficking and domestic violence.

Bangladesh is one of the many countries in the world where violence against women and trafficking are both wide-spread. Instances of violence against women such as physical abuse, rape, killing, forced prostitution, trafficking for sex and sex tourism, battering, kidnapping, sexual harassment, and acid-throwing are common. Oxfam GB works to fight the causes and consequences of trafficking in Bangladesh.

Oxfam's emergency interventions in Bangladesh often include some provision for the prevention of trafficking. For example, after the heavy rains during September 2000, when water coming from West Bengal resulted in unexpected floods in south-west and north-west Bangladesh, destroying local people's livelihoods, Oxfam offered support. People in these regions were severely affected. As livelihoods were destroyed there was little capacity to cope with the serious impacts of the flooding. Interruption of education, erosion of incomes, and the migration of income earners all raised the risk of trafficking of adolescents. In response, Oxfam implemented a programme that, in addition to funding rehabilitation initiatives, focused on agriculture, cash for work, winter clothes distribution, rebuilding housing and sanitation, and advocacy initiatives to raise awareness and minimise the risk of trafficking.

Oxfam GB recognises that the consequences of trafficking of women and girls are exacerbated by gender biases in institutions. Oxfam GB attempted to address this problem through support for Naripokkho, a women's organisation founded in 1983 that works for the advancement of women's rights. Naripokkho is a membership organisation undertaking advocacy, research, and training on various issues related to women's rights and development. Violence against women has been a priority concern from its very inception. The program supported by Oxfam monitors state mechanisms and tries to institutionalise a process of state accountability for the prevention and reduction of violence against women, including trafficking.

Examples from Nepal are also useful because they demonstrate a more systematic approach to supporting local organisations to combat trafficking.

Oxfam's anti-trafficking work in Nepal

While there has been no systematic research to determine the true extent of trafficking in women in Nepal, observers believe that most Nepali women are trafficked to India, the Middle East, and other Asian countries primarily for sex work. It is estimated that there are more than 200,000 Nepalese women in Indian brothels, with additional tens of thousands of Nepalese women in other countries who have been forced into sex work or other work in oppressive situations and inhumane conditions each year (Child Worker in Nepal Concerns Centre [CWIN] 1992).

Nepal is beset with many socio-economic problems, and the extreme poverty in some regions facilitates the trafficking of women and girls. More than 70 per cent of Nepalis live below the poverty line. The average per capita annual income is US$180. There is widespread illiteracy, especially among women, 72 per cent of whom are illiterate (Central Bureau of Statistics 2000).

The flourishing trade in women is influenced by the socio-economic context. Some rural families experience great difficulties in trying to sustain themselves. While the deteriorating socio-economic conditions affect all members of society, women in particular are vulnerable to trafficking due to the discrimination they face in household decision-making matters, and the constraints they face with regard to viable opportunities for earning a living. Families' vulnerability to the trafficking of their female members is a symptom of the desperation that exists. Socio-cultural pressures marginalise women from birth onwards, and once a woman has been forced into sex slavery, there is no going back.

Traffickers often use family members and close friends of targeted women and girls to lure them and avoid detection by authorities or communities as demonstrated by the case of Bimala (in the Sindhupalchock district, 40 km north east of Kathmandu). Bimala and Nanu Maya were good friends, studying together in grade eight at a local school. Traffickers managed to convince Nanu to lure her friend to go to Kathmandu, with the promise of better education and a job, without informing her family. The organisation Gramin Mahila Srijansheel Pariwar (an Oxfam partner) managed to rescue Bimala from Kathmandu and return her to her family. While Nanu and her mother were prosecuted, the real traffickers escaped justice.

The aim of the Oxfam programme in Nepal is to reduce trafficking in women and to work towards making a positive impact on the lives of women. In practice, the programme has increasingly focused on two aspects of anti-trafficking work: educating communities on the mechanisms and consequences of trafficking, and supporting the enforcement of existing laws and the formulation of appropriate policies, laws, and conventions to combat trafficking. Programme activities range from the grassroots to national, regional (in South Asia), and global levels. This integrated multi-level approach aims to address the problem of violation of women's rights during the recruitment, work, and rescue stages of trafficking, as well as the institutional aspects.

At grassroots level, the work focuses on collaboration with various institutions to educate communities, and to support survivors through legal processes against traffickers. Sindhupalchock is one of the most remote of Nepal's 75 districts, with a large ethnic minority population. It is located in the central hilly region of Nepal, and shares its northern border with Tibet. Since this is one of the poorest districts in the country and among the most vulnerable to trafficking, Oxfam GB has been working here with two local organisations managed and controlled by women, and with the District Development Committee, since 1998.

At the national level, the work is directed towards alliance building among relevant NGOs and advocacy groups to promote law enforcement and reform based on international human rights conventions. At the regional level, Oxfam has worked with several of its partners, and more specifically with the Alliance Against Trafficking in Women (AATWIN) and the Asian Women Human Rights Council (AWHRC) as well as other regional feminist groups, to lobby the South Asian Association for Regional Co-operation (SAARC) to set up regional mechanisms (e.g. regional courts) to address the issue bilaterally.

At the international level, our priority has been to work with international feminist groups and advocacy networks (e.g. Global Alliance against Trafficking in Women [GAATW] and the Asian Women Human Rights Council [AWHRC]) to tackle trafficking issues within the UN, including the optional protocol.

This contextual and multi-layered approach has been successful in some areas. The Annual Impact Report, prepared by Oxfam GB (Oxfam GB 2001) summarises some of the changes that have taken place since the programme started. There are overall improvements in the participation of women in formal politics. The five major political parties in Nepal have accepted that women should have 33 per cent seats in parliamentary structures, as against 20 per cent (in village development committees), and five per cent (House of Representatives). Women's groups are lobbying to have women's names lodged as heads of household, along with men's, during the national census planned for June. Women are also starting to come forward as candidates for the next district elections.

The incidence of trafficking has decreased by about 15 per cent in Sindhupalchock district, as a result of legal action and campaigning against the traffickers. One hundred and fifty cases of violence against women and 75 trafficking cases have been registered. Several cases have been heard by village and district development committees, and perpetrators of violence and trafficking have been punished.

Conclusions

Trafficking in women is a complex and extremely sensitive phenomenon, inextricably linked to poverty, migration, work, sex, money, and violence. Oxfam's work in Nepal and in other countries provides examples of a pragmatic but principled approach to the problem.

Notes

1 Over the years, there has been much debate about the definition of 'trafficking'. Even with the introduction of the Trafficking Protocol in 2001, disagreement remains about the interpretation of the trafficking as set out in the Protocol.
2 Not her real name.
3 Shakti Shamuha is a campaign organisation formed by survivors, and an Oxfam partner.

Meena Poudel is a development anthropologist and feminist activist currently working as Programme Representative for Oxfam GB in Nepal, GPO Box 2500, Kathmandu, Nepal. E-mail: mpoudel@oxfam.org.np

Ines Smyth is a Policy Adviser for Oxfam GB, 274 Banbury Road, Oxford OX2 7DZ, United Kingdom. E-mail: ismyth@oxfam.org.uk

References

Asia Watch (1993) *A Modern Form of Slavery: Trafficking of Women and Girls into Brothels in Thailand*, New York: Asia Watch

Central Bureau of Statistics (2000) *Statistical Pocket Book*, Kathmandu: Central Bureau of Statistics, National Planning Commission

Child Worker in Nepal Concerns Centre (CWIN) (1992) *Bal Sarokar*, Kathmandu: CWIN

Oxfam GB (2001) 'South Asia Annual Impact Report', June 2001, Oxford: Oxfam GB

Oxfam GB (2002) 'Achieving Maximum Impact: Oxfam's Strategy for Overcoming Poverty', Oxford: Oxfam GB

Resources

Compiled by Nittaya Thiraphouth

Publications

Human Rights and Trafficking in Persons: A Handbook (2001), Global Alliance Against Trafficking in Women, International Co-ordination Office, PO Box 36, Bangkok Noi Office, Bangkok 10700, Thailand.

This handbook is intended for NGOs, activists, and others who come into contact with trafficked persons or who are interested in the issue of trafficking. This is a broad-based manual, containing general strategies that can be further adapted to local contexts. The handbook was developed out of regional human rights training held for activists in Asia, Eastern Europe, Africa, and Latin America. In GAATW's 1999 global meeting to evaluate the regional human rights trainings, participants from each of the trainings agreed that defining specific actions against trafficking is very dependent upon the regional context.

Handbook for Human Rights Action (in the Context of Traffic in Women) (1996), GAATW.

This handbook is the result of an international workshop on human rights, conducted in June 1996 in Bangkok by GAATW, in conjunction with the Foundation For Women, Thailand, and the International Human Rights Law Group, USA. The handbook provides knowledge about the practical use of UN human rights mechanisms in order to combat traffic in women, and to increase political action on national and international levels. It is a compilation of different types of materials, from descriptions and definitions of terminology to the texts of relevant UN documents.

Human Rights in Practice; A Guide to Assist Trafficked Women and Children (1997), GAATW.

This manual, the result of a collaborative effort, is intended to be a resource for women's and children's rights organisations that are either already involved in assisting trafficked women and children or are intending to do so. It also aims to strengthen the political and lobbying efforts of NGOs to influence national and international policies to promote the rights of women and children who are trafficked or vulnerable to being trafficked. In order to ensure its accessibility amongst a wide group of community workers, this manual will soon be translated into other languages.

Stopping Forced Labour: Global Report under the Follow Up to the ILO Declaration on Fundamental Principles and Rights at Work (2001), International Labour Office, CH-1211, Geneva 22, Switzerland. Available on-line at: http://www.ilo.org/declaration

This Global Report is the follow up to the 1998 ILO Declaration on the Fundamental Principles and Rights at Work, and is principally aimed at policy makers and practitioners. Part One examines the forms of slavery most prevalent in the world today, and includes considerable analysis of bonded labour in South Asia. Part Two assesses the efforts of the ILO and other international agencies to prevent these forms of forced labour and to rehabilitate its victims. Part Three presents an action plan for the future. The report also contains a series of questions to be discussed by the International Labour Conference.

Crossing Borders: Against Trafficking in Women and Girls, A Resource Book for Working against Trafficking in the Baltic Sea Region (1999), Kvinnoforum, Kungsgatan 65, SE-111 22 Stockholm, Sweden. Available on-line at:
http://www.qweb.kvinnoforum.se/misc/ResourceBookBody-Nov99.rtf

Produced by Kvinnoforum, a Swedish organisation working to promote gender equity, this book provides general background information about trafficking, describes different approaches to the problem, shares knowledge about victims of trafficking, and describes the results of Kvinnoforum's work. To facilitate the building of networks, the resource book lists more than 80 Baltic and Nordic organisations working against trafficking, or interested in incorporating this work into their current activities.

Disposable People: New Slavery in the Global Economy (1999), Kevin Bales, University of California Press, Berkeley, CA 94720, USA.

Written in accessible narrative style, this is an investigation into the current global resurgence of slavery. The author draws on interviews with victims, perpetrators, and public officials to describe slavery in its modern form, and the way in which it has adapted to the global economy. Different chapters focus on practices in particular countries, such Thailand, Mauritania, Brazil, Pakistan, India, and parts of America and Europe. The conclusion offers suggestions for how individuals and governments can combat slavery, and describes successful anti-slavery actions by international and local organisations.

Enslaved People in the 1990s: A Report by Anti-Slavery International in Collaboration with IWGIA (1997), Anti-Slavery International, The Stableyard, Broomgrove Road, London, SW9 9TL, UK, and International Work Group for Indigenous Affairs, Fiolstraede 10, DK-1171, Copenhagen, Denmark.

This report looks at different forms of slavery and slavery-like practices and their consequences. It comprises a collection of case studies from Asia and South America that focus on the slavery and exploitation of indigenous people, and argues that slavery affects indigenous people differently, attacks their whole collective identity, and threatens their survival as a people.

Sex Slaves: The Trafficking of Women in Asia (2000), Louise Brown, Virago Press, Bretten House, Lancaster place, London WC2E 7EN, UK.

The outcome of intimate interviews with sex workers and others involved in the sex industry including NGOs and government officials, this book provides an insight into the experience of sex workers forced into the trade, describing their journey from their homes to their lives in brothels. It covers different aspects of the trafficking trade, the market for prostitution, and explores the identities of agents and customers. The author overwhelmingly finds that the primary customers of sex workers are in fact not Western but Asian men, and argues that in rigidly structured Asian societies where repressive sexual codes are built on the subjugation of women, 'sex and slavery are absolutely inseparable'. Its narrative style is suitable for a wide audience.

Making the Harm Visible: Global Sexual Exploitation of Women and Girls, Speaking Out and Providing Services (1999), Donna M. Hughes and Claire M. Roche (eds), Coalition Against Trafficking in Women, University of Massachusetts, PO Box 9338, N. Amherst, MA 01059, USA. Available online at:
http://www.uri.edu/artsci/wms/hughes/mhvint.htm

Making the Harm Visible is a collection of writings on the global sexual exploitation of women and girls by survivors, activists, and service providers. The 44 pieces from Asia, Africa, Europe, South America, the Caribbean, North America, and the Middle East offer personal, insightful, and challenging perspectives on sexual violence and prostitution. They reveal a spectrum of violence and exploitation from a variety of cultures and contexts, with the main focus on how prostitution industries objectify and exploit women and girls. These accounts and reports describe how women are resisting the violence done to them as individuals and to other women and girls in their communities by organising protests, building programs and movements, and providing services to stop the violence, heal the harm, and prevent future exploitation.

Owed Justice: Thai Women Trafficked into Debt Bondage in Japan (2000), Human Rights Watch, 350 Fifth Avenue, 34th Floor, New York, NY 10118-3299, USA.

This report is the outcome of extensive research over a period of six years by Human Rights Watch in co-operation with local organisations and researchers on the trafficking of women from Thailand to Japan. It traces the experiences of women trafficked as 'hostesses' from recruitment to travel and subsequent employment, and examines the response of the respective governments and the international community, concluding with targeted recommendations.

The Traffic in Women: Human Realities of the Sex Trade (1997), Siriporn Skrobanek, Nattaya Boonpakdi, and Chutma Janthakeero, Zed Books, 7 Cynthia Street, London N1 9JK, UK.

This moving but unemotional account of the rapidly-expanding international traffic in women reveals it as a global issue. Using original, carefully-documented field studies from Thailand, it explores the nature and extent of the problem worldwide. It demonstrates how traffic in women and forced prostitution are aspects of transnational migration, and how these women also suffer grave violations of human rights. The book also shows how women themselves can be empowered to end trafficking, and ends with detailed recommendations for change.

Global Sex Workers: Rights, Resistance and Redefinition (1998), Kamala Kempadoo and Jo Doezema (eds), Routledge, 29 West 35th Street, New York, NY 1000, USA.

Combining scholarly essays with personal narratives, interviews, and reports, and situating sex workers as working people who should enjoy human rights and workers' rights, this book reveals how ordinary women and men in prostitution define and shape their struggle for social change and justice. Includes a bibliography and list of contributing organisations.

Prostitution, Power and Freedom (1991), Julia O'Connell Davidson, University of Michigan Press, PO Box 1104, Ann Arbor, MI 48106-1104, USA.

Prostitution, Power and Freedom brings new insights to the ongoing debate among scholars, activists, and others on the controversial subject of prostitution. Sociologist Julia O'Connell Davidson's study is based on wide research from all over the world and includes interviews with prostitutes, clients, and procurers active in the international sex trade. The author demonstrates the complexity of prostitution, arguing that it is not simply an effect of male oppression and violence or insatiable sexual needs; nor is it an unproblematic economic encounter. The book provides a sophisticated understanding that uncovers the economic and political inequalities underlying prostitution, but also shows that while prostitution necessarily implies certain freedoms for the clients, the amount of freedom experienced by individual prostitutes varies greatly.

Crime and Servitude: An Exposé of the Traffic in Women for Prostitution from the Newly Independent States (1997), Gillian Caldwell, Steven Galster, and Nadia Steinzor, Global Survival Network, PO Box 73214, Washington, DC, USA. Available on-line at: http://www.globalsurvival.net/femaletrade/9711rsussia.html

This thorough report details the findings of a two-year investigation by the Global Survival Network into the trafficking of women from Russia and the former Soviet Union for prostitution. As well as interviews and information collected from NGOs, law enforcement agencies, and trafficked women themselves, one research method used by GSN was to establish a dummy company in the USA that purported to specialise in importing foreign women as escorts and entertainers. This facilitated access to the operations of international trafficking networks, traffickers, and their partners. The report targets several 'receiving' countries and concludes with recommendations for action and policies for preventing traffickers and providing assistance to their victims.

The Sex Sector: The Economic and Social Bases of Prostitution in South-East Asia (1998), Lin Lean Lim (ed.), International Labour Office.

This collection comprises country case studies from Indonesia, Malaysia, the Philippines, and Thailand, but has relevance for many countries with a significant sex industry. Each study covers the respective historical, social, economic, and legislative contexts, and demonstrates that prostitution has social components relating to unequal power relations between men and women, as well as children and adults. Authors examine the different modes of entry into prostitution and the possibility of making a distinction between voluntary and coerced prostitution. It includes a separate chapter on child prostitution. The book concludes with a discussion of policy and programme lessons, and advocates for the elimination of child prostitution.

Stolen Lives: Trading Women into Sex and Slavery (1996), Sietske Altink, The Haworth Press Inc., 10 Alice St., Binghamton, NY 13904, USA.

Examines how women are hired in their home country and transported, left without money, passports, or permits, and how they become trapped in prostitution and domestic slavery. Includes women's testimonies, explores international crime networks which exploit women, and exposes the lack of action at regional, national, and international levels.

Profiting from Abuse: An Investigation into the Sexual Exploitation of our Children (2001), UNICEF, 3 United Nations Plaza, New York, NY 10017, USA. Available on-line at: http://www.unicef.org/pubsgen/profiting/profiting.pdf

This report presents the stories of children and young people from all over the world who are involved in the sex trade, as well as the informed opinions of various personalities and authorities committed to ending it. It concludes that education and raising awareness are vital to achieving this, and calls for laws that promote the welfare of children and protect them from abuse. Accessibly written and emotive, it is aimed at governments, law enforcers, and international agencies, as well as civil society organisations.

Children of Other Worlds: Exploitation in the Global Market (2001), Jeremy Seabrook, Pluto Press, 345 Archway Road, London N6 5AA, UK.

Academic in style and structure, this book argues that child labour, like poverty and inequality, is structurally part of globalisation. As its basis, it uses a comparison between industrial Britain in the early nineteenth century and present day Bangladesh.

The Human Rights of Street and Working Children (1998), Iain Bryne, ITDG Publications Ltd., 103-105 Southampton Row, London WC1B 4HH, UK.

Written both for experienced advocates and for non-specialists in the field, this manual explains how to use regional and international treaties and mechanisms for the protection of street and working children when national laws fail. The manual is presented in an accessible question-and-answer format, and is divided into three chapters: defining substantive rights; practical guidelines on how to use regional and international human rights systems; and a list of human rights documents by country.

Child Labour: Targeting the Intolerable (1998), International Labour Organisation. Available on-line at: http://www.ilo.org/public/english/standards/ipec/publ/clrep96.htm

Submitted to ILO member states, this report is aimed at governments, employers, and workers' organisations as part of the ILO campaign to eliminate child labour. *Targeting the Intolerable* draws on the experience of the ILO to chronicle the exploitation and abuse of working children, survey international and national law, and make recommendations for practical action through the adoption of international standards. It also includes a questionnaire to solicit the view of governments on the proposals.

What Works for Working Children (1998), Jo Boyden, Birgitta Ling, and William Myers, Rädda Barnen, Save the Children Sweden, S-107 88 Stockholm, Sweden.

Written from a child-centred perspective, this book reviews and summarises recent research and experience regarding child work, and the processes of child development as they relate to work. It questions widespread concepts and approaches to work and childhood, and offers alternatives. This book is targeted particularly at organisations and practitioners working with children.

Domestic Child Workers: Selected Case Studies on the Situation of the Girl-Child Domestic Workers (1997), Barbara Ojoo, Sinaga Women and Child Labour Resource Centre, PO Box 71991, Nairobi, Kenya.

This study draws primarily on research carried out at the Sinaga Centre, a Kenyan NGO that supports domestic child workers through integrated awareness-raising and rehabilitation programmes. Commissioned by Oxfam Kenya, in collaboration with the Sinaga Centre, the study examines the socio-economic factors that lead to domestic child work, describes working conditions, and raises policy issues for considerations by policy makers and practitioners working on child labour issues.

Early Marriage, Child Spouses (2001), UNICEF, Innocenti Research Centre, Piazza SS. Annunziata 12, 50122 Florence, Italy.

Part of UNICEF's Innocenti Digest series, this issue focuses on early marriage, and comprises a collection of short articles covering the causes, contexts, and impacts of child marriage. It incorporates guidelines for organisations working to end the practice of early marriage, including an article on working toward gender equity in marriage. With the aim of raising awareness among governments and civil society, and of stimulating action, it concludes with a call for more rights-based research on the issue.

Servile Forms of Marriage: Women and Property (1995), Anti-Slavery International.

This paper was prepared for the UN Fourth World Conference on Women in Beijing, in order to bring to the fore the issue of women's property rights and to advocate for the ratification of the Convention on the Elimination of All Forms of Discrimination Against Women. It presents information from published and unpublished reports by NGOs, academics, and others, and uses case studies that were specifically carried out for Anti-Slavery International in Gambia, Tanzania, and Pakistan. The studies focus on family law, property rights, and the division of assets.

Organisations

Anti-Slavery International, Thomas Clarkson House, The Stableyard, Broomgrove Road, London SW9 9TL, UK.
Tel: +44 (0) 20 7501 8920; fax: +44 (0) 20 7738 4110; E-mail: info@antislavery.org
http://www.antislavery.org/

Anti-Slavery International was set up in 1839 with the objective of ending slavery throughout the world. It works with partner organisations around the world to collect information on the issues central to their work: traditional slavery, child labour, bonded labour; and the trafficking and enslavement of men, women, and children. It publishes this information to inform the public and policy makers about slavery issues around the world, and works through international bodies in order to promote laws to protect those exploited by these practices.

Ban Ying, Anklamer Strasse, 10115 Berlin, Germany.
Tel: +49 (0) 30 440 63 73 74;
fax: +49 (0) 30 440 63 75;
E-mail: Ban-Ying@ipn-b.comlink.apc.org
http://www.ban-ying.de/ebanying.htm

Ban Ying was founded in 1988 through the initiative of social workers staffing a Berlin counselling centre for sexually transmitted diseases and AIDS. *Ban Ying* is Thai for 'house of women'. The organisation comprises two projects, a shelter and a co-ordination centre for women from South-East Asia.

CHANGE, Room 222, Bon Marche Centre, 241-51 Ferndale Road, London SW9 8BJ, UK.
Tel: +44 (0) 20 7733 9928; fax: +44 (0) 20 7733 9923; E-mail: change@sister.com
http://www.antitrafficking.org

CHANGE is a woman's human rights organisation based in London, operating with and through contacts all over the world. Its purpose is to promote and protect women's human rights worldwide, and to effect change in all aspects of women's lives including: poverty, violence, access to democracy, and access to economic decision making. It fulfils its aims through research programmes, dissemination of information, and lobbying and training of other organisations and individuals. Change is undertaking an anti-trafficking programme.

Coalition to Abolish Slavery and Trafficking (CAST), Little Tokyo Service Center, 231 E. 3rd St., Suite G104, Los Angeles, California 90013, USA.
Tel: +1 213 473 1611; fax: +1 213 473 1601;
E-mail: cast@trafficked-women.org
http://www.trafficked-women.org/

CAST is an alliance of non-profit service providers, grassroots advocacy groups, and activists dedicated to providing services and human rights advocacy to victims of modern-day slavery. CAST was founded in 1998 in the aftermath of the El Monte sweatshop case. Its mission is to assist persons trafficked for the purpose of forced labour and slavery-like practices, and to work toward ending all instances of such human rights violations.

Coalition Against Trafficking in Women, Dr. Janice Raymond, Co-Executive Director, Coalition Against Trafficking in Women, University of Massachusetts, PO Box 9338, N. Amherst, MA 01059, USA.
Fax: +1 413 367 9262
http://www.catwinternational.org

The Coalition Against Trafficking in Women is a feminist human rights NGO that works internationally to oppose all forms of sexual exploitation.

Committee Against Modern Slavery, 4 Place de Valois, 75001 PARIS, France.
Tel: +33 1 55 35 36 55; fax : +33 1 55 35 36 56; E-mail: ccem@imaginet.fr
http://www.ccem-antislavery.org/

The Committee Against Modern Slavery is a member of 'Article Premier', a collective of 33 NGOs, founded after the 50th Anniversary of the Universal Declaration of Human Rights, and whose aim is to reaffirm the universality and indivisibility of human rights.

Dutch Foundation Against Trafficking in Women (STV), PO Box 1455, 3500 BL UTRECHT, The Netherlands.
Tel: +31 30 716044; fax: +31 30 716084;
E-mail: fe@stv.vx.xs4all.nl
http://www.bayswan.org/FoundTraf.html

The Dutch Foundation Against Trafficking in Women (STV) was initiated in the early 1980s in response to the then highly-publicised issue of sex tourism. It provides support and assistance, advocacy, training, and information sharing.

ECPAT International, 328 Phaya Thai Road, Bangkok 10400, Thailand.
Tel: +662 215 3388; fax +662 215 8272;
E-mail: info@ecpat.net
http://www.ecpat.net

ECPAT is a network of organisations and individuals working together for the elimination of child prostitution, child pornography, and trafficking of children for sexual purposes. It seeks to encourage the world community to ensure that children everywhere enjoy their fundamental rights free from all forms of commercial sexual exploitation.

Global Alliance Against Trafficking in Women, International Co-ordination Office, PO Box 36, Bangkok Noi Office, Bangkok 10700, Thailand.
Tel: +662 864 1427 8; fax: +662 864 1637;
E-mail: gaatw@mozart.inet.co.th
http://www.inet.co.th/org/gaatw/

The Global Alliance Against Traffic in Women (GAATW) was formed at the International Workshop on Migration and Traffic in Women held in Chiang Mai, Thailand in October 1994. Since that time, GAATW has grown into a movement of organisations and individuals worldwide, and has coordinated, organised, and facilitated work on issues related to trafficking in persons and women's labour migration in virtually every region of the world.

Global March Against Child Labour, L-6, Kalkaji, New Delhi 19, India.
Tel: +91 11 6224899, 6475481; fax: +91 11 6236818; E-mail: childhood@globalmarch.org
http://www.globalmarch.org/

Global March is involved in assessing and lobbying for the ratification and implementation of the ILO Convention Against the Worst forms of Child Labour.

International Labour Organisation, International Programme on the Elimination of Child Labour.
Tel: +41 22 799 8181; fax: +41 22 799 8771;
E-mail: ipec@ilo.org
http://www.ilo.org/public/english/standards/ipec/index.htm

IPEC's aim is to work towards the progressive elimination of child labour by strengthening national capacities to address child labour problems, and by creating a worldwide movement to combat it.

International Organization for Migration (IOM), 17 Route des Morillons, CP 71, CH-1211 Geneva 19, Switzerland.
Tel: +41 22 717 9111; fax: 41 22 798 6150;
E-mail: info@iom.int
http://www.iom.int

Established in 1951 as an intergovernmental organisation to resettle European displaced persons, refugees, and migrants, IOM now encompasses a variety of migration management activities throughout the world, including measures to counter trafficking in persons.

La Strada (a contact list by country is available at http://www.ecn.cz/lastrada)

La Strada is an international program that operates in the Netherlands, Poland, Bulgaria, Czech Republic, Macedonia, Moldova, Bosnia and Herzegovina, Belarus, and Ukraine. It focuses on prevention of traffic in women, support of victims of trafficking, influencing legislation, and disseminating information.

Network of Sex Work Projects, 3 Morley Rd. Observatory, 7925 Cape Town, South Africa.
E-mail: sexworknet@ct.stormnet.co.za
http://www.walnet.org/csis/groups/nswp/

NSWP is an informal alliance that participates in independently financed projects in partnership with member organisations and technical support agencies.

Electronic resources

Qweb
http://www.qweb.kvinnoforum.se/trafficking

This worldwide network on women's health and gender issues runs a networking project against trafficking. The site contains a number of references, online documents, links, and details of 250 members with special interest in trafficking.

Stop-Traffic
E-mail: ingsn@igc.apc.org
http://www.stop-traffic.org

Launched by the Global Survival Network in March 1998, Stop-Traffic is a facilitated international electronic mailing list that deals with human rights abuses associated with trafficking in persons, with an emphasis on trafficking in women for forced prostitution/sexual slavery, sweatshop labour, domestic service, and coercive mail-order bride arrangements.

United Nations Office for Drug Control and Crime Prevention
http://www.odccp.org/

Contains on-line access to key policy documents such as the UN Convention Against Transnational Organised Crime and other supporting documents.

Videos

Bought and Sold (1997), Witness, 353 Broadway, New York, NY 1001, USA.
http://www.witness.org

Witness partners at The Global Survival Network (GSN) conducted a two-year investigation to uncover the growing international transport of Russian women for prostitution. In addition to interviewing NGOs, women who had been trafficked abroad, and police and government officials in many countries, GSN established a dummy company based in the USA that purportedly specialised in importing foreign women as escorts and entertainers. Under that guise, GSN gained entry to the shadowy operations of international trafficking and produced this documentary film, which gives an insider's perspective on how the international trade in women actually works.

Out of Sight, Out of Mind (1999), Anti-Slavery International.

This 15-minute video was produced by Anti-Slavery as part of its campaign on child domestic workers in the Philippines. Made with local NGO forum Visayan, this video was shown on TV and in Congress in the Philippines. This has led to the drafting of a new law which will protect child domestic workers. Contact the Publications Officer: b.smaga@antislavery.org for further information.

Sisters and Daughters Betrayed, The Global Fund for Women, 425 Sherman Avenue, Suite 300, Palo Alto, CA 94306, USA.

This video about the realities of sex trafficking and forced prostitution was released in1995 by independent video-maker Chela Blitt. It examines the economics of trafficking and the parallels between the situation in Asia and other regions. It presents interviews with activist women in Asia who are involved in campaigns against trafficking.

The Child Brides: Early and Forced Marriage (1998), Umbrella Pictures for Channel 4, available from Anti-Slavery International.

Shot on location in Ethiopia, this programme reveals how many young girl are taken from their homes and are forced to marry. Unable to finish school, they often become pregnant, and face serious consequences to their health and well-being.

Conferences

Conference on Trafficking in Persons in Asia: The Human Rights Challenge of Globalisation, Hawaii, USA, Spring 2002.

With plenary sessions and 'hands-on' workshops, the practical focus of the conference will build on monitoring and implementing two existing international initiatives to combat and prevent trafficking: the Asian Regional Initiative Against Trafficking in Women and Children (ARIAT) Plan of Action; and the UN Protocol to Prevent, Suppress and Punish Trafficking in Persons. For further information, contact Dr. Nancie Caraway, Globalization Research Centre, Director of Women's Human Rights Projects, 1580 Makaloa Street, Suite 970, Honolulu, Hawaii 96822, USA. Tel: +1 808 945 1450, ext. 106; fax: +1 808 945 1455;
E-mail: nancie@hawaii.edu